Operation

Ark

Pen Farthing

CLARET PRESS

Copyright © Pen Farthing, 2024
The moral right of the author has been asserted.

ISBN paperback: 978-1-910461-70-9
ISBN ebook: 978-1-910461-71-6

A CIP catalogue record for this book is available from the British Library.

This paperback can be ordered from all bookstores as well as from Amazon, and the ebook is available on online platforms such as Amazon and iBooks.

Cover and Interior Design by Petya Tsankova

www.claretpress.com

Claret Press

To the amazingly kind and generous people from all over the world who donated to ensure Operation Ark was a success by not looking the other way.

You believed in us – you made the difference.

I will be forever grateful.

Thank you.

People and animals

Pen F

Contents

Part 1:
Introduction

Without fail I would rush home from school every afternoon to eagerly watch BBC news during 1982. Max Hastings was reporting on the harrowing events as British Royal Marines of 3 Commando Brigade "yomped" across the Falkland Islands in harsh winter conditions to fight through well dug-in Argentine positions, reclaiming them from the invading Argentine forces.

Right there and then, thirteen-year-old me knew that when I grew up, I too was going to be a Royal Marine Commando. There was no doubt. Overcoming the toughest infantry training in the world became my driving force.

The careers office promotional material of a troop sergeant leading his men in combat during the Falklands just inspired me. The respect and responsibility he had for those thirty young Marines triggered something in me. I never looked back, even when my application to join up as an officer was turned down. I didn't give up. I applied to join as a non-commissioned rank and work my way up from the bottom. Nobody and nothing was going to stop me from becoming a Royal Marine Commando.

I passed out with 550 Troop on the 30th of September 1988 as a fully-fledged Royal Marine Commando and was awarded the King's Badge, the best all-round recruit in training.

Some twelve years later, 9/11 happened.

The coalition of Western countries led by the United States invaded Afghanistan to remove the Taliban from power and hunt down those responsible for the atrocities that had befallen America.

And in 2006 I was deployed as the troop sergeant for 5 Troop, Kilo Company, 42 Commando Royal Marines, surrounded by Taliban in the remote desert outpost of "Now

Zad", deep in Helmand province. The young Marines on their first tour of duty were my responsibility. To this day I can recall that photo of the troop sergeant with his Marines that had inspired me all those years prior in the careers office in Chelmsford. That tour of duty shattered any romantic notion of what real responsibility meant. It meant tough choices and sucking up any personal concerns.

It was war. Not all of my young lads came home. It was brutal and dark. Handing a grieving mother the Union Jack flag that had been draped over her son's coffin will live with me forever.

Bizarrely, that tour of duty in Afghanistan set the scene for where we are now.

It was there when I realised my path lay not in a military solution but amongst the Afghan people, working with them. A dog I rescued from the chaos of that tour of duty, whom I named Nowzad, paved the way for the charity to be born. I just followed.

Nowzad is Dari for "newborn". Nowzad, the charity, had been operating in Afghanistan since 2007. We built our charity from the ground up during the worst years of the conflict with no military protection. We lived outside the wire, in a residential area of Kabul. We had no protection except for the four dry mud walls that formed the outer perimeter of our clinic and house.

We were not the only Westerners. Brave and dedicated soldiers from the coalition of countries, determined to see positive change in Afghanistan, gave everything over a twenty-year period to be the difference for future generations of young Afghans. And those Afghans seized the opportunities offered. Universities across the country, particular in Herat and Kabul, were oversubscribed. According to UNESCO, over 100,000 girls were in some form of education across the country at the start of 2021, compared to just 5,000 when the coalition removed the Taliban from power in 2001.

The Taliban movement had come to power in the mid-90s, bringing a severe and unforgiving form of Islam rarely seen anywhere else in the world. Most people believe that Afghanistan has always been a strict Islamic country. Nothing could be further from the truth.

Marnie, once a good friend until charity politics intervened, went to university in Kabul as a young American girl. She showed me a photo once of her riding her bike to university during the mid-seventies. The striking feature of the grainy black and white photo is that Marnie is wearing a miniskirt. No women were wearing any form of headscarf in the other photos she showed me.

Nowzad had immediately looked to employ the first-ever female Afghan veterinarians. We worked extremely hard to promote young women's rights by ensuring our staff was over 25% female. They seamlessly joined our determined team promoting animal welfare in a country slowly rebuilding itself.

I was proud to be just a small part of that. I was happy.

And then August 2021 happened: the chaotic withdrawal of Western forces from Afghanistan. I found myself needing to evacuate my Afghan staff and the animals we cared for.

This book describes those events as they occurred and is fact. I was there. I lived it. Breathed it. Escaped it.

Everything you are about to read happened exactly as I have described it. I am extremely keen not to be sued. That's quite the incentive to be accurate.

Everything in this book comes from the memory of myself and other eyewitnesses, backed up by the photographs I took as things happened, which are clearly dated and time-stamped with the location. More details come from the various WhatsApp groups that we used to plan and eventually implement Operation Ark.

I am not going to focus too much on the political happenings at the time, so if you are hoping on some revealing gossip about Boris Johnson, his wife Carrie, Ben Wallace, or even Peter Quentin, well, there is none. I never had any to begin with.

I am also not going to focus on dogs either. They were part of the plan but never *the* plan.

Members of parliament, journalists, social media commentators, and even a civil servant from a select committee hearing had no idea what was really happening or had happened to me on the ground during those two weeks of August 2021. Yet they made statements of "fact". Why they did it, I don't know. I just know that no one took two minutes to ponder what their "fact" would do to me.

That "fact" would then become the new "truth". But it was a lie of offensive and damaging proportions. Let's put it straight: It was never ever "pets over people".

That tagline was just awful. Yet that was the stick they used to beat me with – and the ethos of Operation Ark.

Pets over people. Even the choice of the word "pets" was designed entirely to belittle and discredit the fifteen years of tireless work that we had put into building Nowzad as an animal welfare charity in Afghanistan. Fifteen years of saving human lives through our rabies-prevention work for which we have won awards.

Don't get me wrong, I love dogs. Of course I do. Often you will find me in my local pub sporting my favourite T-shirt, an eye-wincing bright-yellow affair with a screen print that reads: "I love dogs and beer and maybe 3 people."

And guess what? My T-shirt is not lying! Especially the "3 people" part.

I would say in my defence that those people I do care for, I am wholly and completely committed to. In fact, I risked my life for them.

In August of 2021, during the chaos of the sudden evacuation of Westerners and their Afghan allies from Kabul, I had the opportunity to make a difference for the people I was responsible for and cared for.

Or I could have just abandoned them.

I could have made a solo run for the airport at any time and just not bothered looking back. Arrived home safely to my adorable wife. For us, the world would have kept turning. No questions asked. No media scrum. No tarnishing of my name.

But I chose to stay, even beyond the potential point of no return. I was, in a way, behind enemy lines because I stayed after the Taliban took over Kabul. I stayed because I am cut from a very different cloth. As a former Royal Marine Commando, I was taught early on that we never abandon the people we serve alongside on the ground. Just because I was no longer a serving Royal Marine and my team were civilians did not mean I had given up the *ethos* of being a Marine.

It was always people *and* animals. Because I could do both.

The aeroplane had a passenger cabin and a cargo hold.

People in the passenger cabin.

Animals in the cargo hold.

It was not rocket science.

But it didn't happen that way. In this book I'll lay out exactly what did happen. And had to happen. And the price I paid for it.

If we had failed then that would have meant committing our Afghan staff and their families to a life of solitude and isolation, forced to live under a dictatorship that denies every fundamental human and democratic right, especially and above all to women.

Yet in saving them, the life I had wished for and dreamed of ended abruptly because of the success of Operation Ark.

I have no choice now but to suck it up and acknowledge that their freedom came at a price I must accept. Freedom always comes at a price and my loss was insignificant to what some willingly sacrifice. I truly believed in what I was doing to help our people at *that moment* in time.

So – as I am constantly asked – would I do it all again?

I think about it briefly but always answer yes. When you have an opportunity to make a positive difference, you need to grab it with both hands. You can pay the ferryman later. The young Afghan girls now able to go to school here in England are testimony to whether or not we did the right thing.

The Operation Ark "escape committee" consisted of fourteen dedicated people, some already associated with our charity, others not. I am only describing the actions of a few as most do not want to be mentioned by name. They managed to stay out of the spotlight and have no wish to be thrust into it now. Some have requested their names be changed or nicknamed.

All of them were crucial to the success of Operation Ark. I am truly so grateful and proud of their commitment to evacuate people who most of them had never met. Every day all of them took part in probably three or four Zoom calls at all hours. David, Jen, Ann, Sam, Dora the Explorer, Ian, Tom, Dan, Nina, Kaisa, Trudy Harrison MP, Pat, Tony, and Peter Egan. Two of the names have been changed as per their request. A thank you is just not enough for what they achieved. I do not need to introduce them, let's just say they are folks with a heart of gold.

There are more aspects to Operation Ark than I have been able to convey in this book. For example, we planned to take the whole shooting match to India: staff, dogs, cats, the lot! Planning was well advanced. I even secured an Indian visa at the height of the withdrawal just before the Indian embassy itself evacuated. But we did not go to India and sadly I just don't have the word count for that story. I could describe the almost comical conversations about attempting to blow a hole in the airport security fence to get in. Yes, we actually were having those conversations with a US security contractor on the inside but sadly that is for another day.

So, this is the story of Operation Ark as I lived it, as our team staggered from one problem to the next, making split-second decisions that were literally life or death to rescue Nowzad's Afghan staff and its animals, and bring them all to a place of safety and peace.

Part 2:
Waiting for the Taliban

May 2021

The van tyres screeched as I turned the plastic steering wheel hard to the left and gunned the vehicle out of the junction without pausing to stop at the faded painted lines. A snatched glance left and right had confirmed there was no traversing traffic. The van's assisted power steering was not the best these days and it required some sturdy manual input to reduce the size of the turning circle and prevent us from veering off into the rusting metal fence railing that ran parallel to the road.

"Hold on!" I yelled over the noise from the open windows of the van, providing the essential cooling breeze against the almost unbearable heat of a Kabul summer. The van's primitive air conditioning system had long ago ceased working.

My passenger leant to the right as the G-force of the turn pulled him.

Once the van had rode through the turn, I applied maximum pedal to the metal and deftly moved the gear stick into fourth before crunching up into fifth. The van gained speed as we headed off along what was now a straight road for at least a quarter of a mile.

We had just left the normally busy "Passport Road" where an Afghan would apply for their passport, and were heading towards a quieter neighbourhood of southern Kabul, not that far from the Nowzad charity's compound.

It had been late in the afternoon when we received the call about a dog covered in mange just a few blocks away from where the Nowzad small animal clinic was located.

Mange is a nasty skin disease that affects mammals and, in Kabul, mostly dogs. Basically, microscopic mites burrow into the animal's skin causing hair loss and red painful dry patches of skin. Unless treated effectively it can become fatal.

Charging headlong out of the clinic, I had grabbed Dr Mujtaba who was Nowzad's senior veterinarian and my very good friend. Together we hastened to the last location the dog had been spotted in. We only had a small window of opportunity to locate it before the dog moved on of its own volition or was chased away by an unfriendly local. This would leave us with little to no chance of finding that poor animal amongst the many narrow mud-built alleyways that dissected sprawling family compounds and buildings.

It was my worst scenario being unable to recover a dog that I knew desperately needed treatment. I felt heartbroken whenever we failed to bring a dog in. I would berate myself that I should have chosen another route, brought more staff, did this or shouldn't have done that. I couldn't bear to see a dog curled up defenceless on the side of the dusty and rubbish-strewn road, scabby patches of pink skin denoting a severe mange attack, and then fail to help it.

Over the years I have put myself in some crazy and probably stupid situations to rescue a sorry-looking dog covered in mange. My priority was always to trap the animal and bring it into the clinic for potentially life-saving treatment that, in the case of mange, took several weeks to administer.

Some dogs were resigned to their fate and would come quietly, even at times walking slowly toward us, allowing us to scoop them up in a blanket and bundle them gently into the prepared travel crate in the back of our van. Others though would not. Those dogs would fight like hell to escape our clutches, screaming like banshees when we were finally able to scoop them up in the net. Happily though, they always came round to our way of thinking after several good meals and some TLC back at the clinic.

In most cases we would treat them, vaccinate them against rabies, neuter or spay them, and release them back where we found them, with an ear clipped to denote that they were part of our TNVR programme. TNVR stands for Trap, Vaccinate, Neuter, and Release, which is a very humane way of reducing the stray dog population in Kabul and preventing the spread of rabies.

But this bloody dog was not making it easy. The chase was on. We had failed at the initial sighting. I had slowly brought the van to stop about 100 yards from where we had spied the dog, curled up and sleeping under a broken donkey cart. Slowly, mimicking Special Forces operatives stalking their prey, we'd ghost-walked towards the unassuming dog, catch pole and net held ready aloft in our hands.

Except we were not Special Forces and the dog was aware of our intentions. She was having none of it.

As my booted foot crunched down on a discarded can of Coca-Cola, the covert game was up. The small dog, bare scabbed pink patches covering her ravaged body, immediately sprung to escape. Like a shot, she scarpered through a gap between Mujtaba and some rubble from a toppled old wall before we could react.

"Get back to the van!" I yelled as we both legged it back the way we'd just came.

We threw the catch pole and net in through the open sliding door. I'd left it open as the door catch was stiff and sometimes not easy to operate. Now we could retrieve the items quickly when we next stopped. I managed to clock the dog had just hightailed it to the left, around the corner of the junction. We shot forward.

"Can you see her?" I yelled. I was too busy concentrating on an overtaking slot opening in front of us so I could manoeuvre around a battered Corolla taking its time and blocking my progress. As the oncoming car passed, I swerved out left and made the overtake.

"There!" Mujtaba exclaimed, pointing excitedly to the pathway on the left.

I just caught a glimpse of dirt-smudged white as the dog dodged between vendors in her haste to find somewhere safe away from people. The little white dog was moving fast. I straightened the wheel and accelerated so we were keeping pace with her.

The van was a very second-hand Indian model which roughly translated as "Princess" if I recall correctly. The front contained the driver's seat (on the left of the vehicle) and a double passenger seat to the right. Currently Mujtaba was sliding across both.

The back of the van was fully windowed. Most vans like this in Kabul contained three rows of seats to fulfil their role as taxis between the villages and settlements outside of the capital. Typically, a driver plus his conductor would ride with the sliding door open, shouting the name of the destination, a cheap way to advertise for paying passengers.

We had long ago removed the passenger seats in the rear to create cargo space. Currently, an unsecured dog travel crate rattled around as I swerved violently, trying to keep the dog in sight. I just hoped it did not bounce out of the open side door. The catch pole, net, and two pairs of loose rabies gloves bounced around along with the crate.

"Grab the net," I yelled. The green meshed net was huge. You could bag a young adult in it if you so chose, the aluminium pole attached to the rim was at least six-foot long.

Mujtaba climbed over the seat and dropped into the back, stretching his arms out to steady himself, wary of being sent spiralling out of the open doorway.

"Once I get alongside the dog, you scoop her up with the net," I explained without looking over my shoulder. The plan seemed simple. I just had to keep pace with the dog and the road up ahead seemed clear enough for the time being to do so.

As I started to glide across the road to keep pace with the dog, I fully expected to see Mujtaba hanging out of the side of the van, catch net in one hand whilst he clung to the grab handle on the side of doorway with the other. I thought he'd be braced in some sort of jousting pose ready to scoop up the wayward dog. I checked my driver's side mirror again.

Still no Mujtaba.

Instead he clambered back over the front seat to sit next to me again.

"It's not the movies, Sir," he said, grinning. We both burst out laughing. He was of course right. And thinking about it, the impact of scooping the dog up, which weighed about 20 kilograms, would have probably ripped Mujtaba's arm from its socket. My bad.

Damn it, though. We were fast approaching the junction ahead which would allow us to join the main Pul-e-Sukhta Road. We needed a new plan. One not straight out of Hollywood.

And the dog happily obliged with one.

Some discarded wooden donkey carts provided a natural shelter for the terrified dog and it skidded to a stop under the nearest trailer, hidden from view by the cart's huge wheels. I drove past the dog and pulled the van over.

As Mujtaba and I exited the vehicle, a familiar voice called out to Mujtaba. Cycling home from work was Basir, our clinic kennel carer. A quiet young Afghan, Basir spoke no English. Father to a young family with a wife he adored, we had gotten lucky when the opportunity arose to employ him as he was a hard worker and never complained. He enjoyed the dogs' company and was meticulous in caring for them, whether cleaning out the kennels or delivering their food.

He pulled up to a stop on a bike that would not have been out of place if my grandad had been riding it thirty years earlier. Basir even had the trouser cycle clips to keep his long Afghan trousers from getting caught in the chain.

As always Basir was smiling. I smiled back and waved. Mujtaba and Basir chatted and then I watched as Basir leant his bike up against the low mud wall that lined the road.

I was hatching a three-pronged attack in my head now that we had our third man for the team. But I shelved it as I watched Basir walk around the side of the van, collect the net and walk further up the road before crossing high above where the dog was hiding. Mujtaba came to join me by the side of the van. We both folded our arms and watched.

Basir turned ninety degrees and wandered back down the side of the road that the mange-covered dog was hiding on. If that had been me and Mujtaba, the dog would have fled by now. Instead, she did nothing.

As Basir walked casually past the parked wooden cart, there was a sudden flurry of activity interspersed with muffled grunts and barking. Basir yelled at the two of us to join him. Mujtaba leant back into the van to retrieve the catch pole. As I arrived at the cart, there was the mange dog, helplessly trapped under the net.

"How the heck did you do that?" I asked Basir knowing full well he had no idea what I was saying. I high-fived him and slapped his back. "Good stuff," I cheered.

Just how the hell he did it will remain a mystery but he confirmed his position as the Nowzad number one dog catcher.

Mujtaba and I jubilantly arrived back at the green-painted double gates that signalled the entrance to the Nowzad charity's compound. From the outside, our compound wall was a dull white colour, and several sections needed repainting as peeling paint patches laid bare the roughly cemented red brick underneath. But that made us blend in with all the other compounds in this neighbourhood that urgently needed attention and that was the way I liked it. We displayed no signage to state it was home to the Nowzad clinic.

It was just a stone's throw away from the only junction along Shura Street. "Shura" in Dari translated as "meeting" and until a few years ago, the parliament of Afghanistan had been housed at the end of the road. Our proximity to such a high-value target had seen us, at times, frenziedly lock down the clinic as Taliban insurgents commenced a surprise attack on the parliamentary estate. We suffered no direct damage but the sound of bullets arcing low over the roof of our house and the not-so-distant thud of a suicide bomber detonating his vest during the opening salvo of an attack was scary enough, thank you very much. We were extremely relieved when the government of India came to the rescue. By way of a contribution towards the rebuilding of Afghanistan, they donated the cost of building a lavish golden-domed palace to serve as the country's new parliament complex located at the end of the famous Darulaman Road, far enough away as to not cause us any concern if it were to be attacked.

The only thing that remained to signify that parliament had once been along our road was a fire station, less than 100 yards from our front gate, built to serve the needs of parliament and still operational. Its heavily gated and fortified entrance, and lack of any outside adornments that we would associate with a fire station, disguised any sign that within those walls were two fully functioning fire trucks. Their shrill sirens and strobing blue lights often pierced the still night air and alerted the local neighbourhood well before they thundered from the compound to answer a call out. Much to our annoyance but seemingly to the delight of the dogs residing within our clinic who always joined in with the cacophony by barking and howling, the Afghan fire crew rushed to whatever emergency had summoned them – maybe a gas cylinder explosion, vehicle accident, household fire, or more commonly these days, devastation caused by a vehicle-borne improvised explosive device (VBIED) exploding.

I waited patiently for our "chowkidor". The peephole opened in the metalled gate and an eyeball scanned our vehicle and the surrounding area. Without acknowledgement the peephole slammed shut. Then came the all-too-familiar metal clunking as the chowkidor lifted the sturdy anti-vehicle bollards from their seating holes. The sound echoed from within the compound gates and drifted out to us on the air of what had been a fierce afternoon of sun.

The gates could now be opened, allowing us to drive the few feet needed until the van's front bumper sat snugly against the far wall within our dull grey-coloured garage. All three sides were formed from heavily reinforced concrete slabs –

specially designed blocks that protected nearly every compound of any importance and that most militaries the world over use to build shelters for protection from incoming mortars. The placement of our blast walls had taken a huge lifting operation involving a knuckle boom crane as each large concrete slab weighed in at over a tonne. Rolls of razor wire lined the top of the slabs.

Whilst expensive, they were, without a doubt, an utter and undeniable necessity to enhance our protection if a suicide bomber or his vehicle were to breach our outer gate. The slab walls would protect us from any blast that occurred within our garage area. The only other exit from the garage security "airlock" was via a small pedestrian gate, blocked by a concrete-filled steel door.

Our multiple layers of security had increased over the years as the security situation had deteriorated. Especially at this time, criminal gangs had become emboldened and their methods and ferocity of attacks were becoming more brazen. If a foreigner was the intended target, then it most likely meant a kidnapping.

My prior military experience dictated that the responsibility for the security of all those living and working inside fell to me, and I was taking no chances with their lives.

When I left the compound, I always strapped on a 9mm pistol. It was a familiar outline in my clothing as I bounded around Kabul with the team. Gaining the license to carry in Afghanistan had been somewhat of a mission and worthy of a book in itself. But suffice to say, carrying it was a responsibility I took extremely seriously. I knew full well that it wouldn't deter a determined Taliban attack, but it might prevent a kidnapping. The fact that over 100 foreigners had been kidnapped from their residences or cars whilst travelling to work during the last ten years weighed heavily on my mind.

The sweat-soaked back of my shirt was stuck to the leather driver's seat. I was looking forward to having a shower and getting changed. As the gates opened inwardly, I carried out one final scan of the road adjacent to either side of the van (currently deserted) and slowly pulled forward through the gates. As the front of the van approached the far wall, I let the vehicle come to a rest and applied the handbrake.

I looked across at Mujtaba and high-fived him. "Welcome to Nowzad," I exclaimed as I killed the engine. He grinned back.

We carried the kennelled-but-terrified dog through the blast gates and to the safety of the other side of the high brick walls, duly topped with yet more razor wire. Security cameras kept watch over every corner of the compound.

Whenever visitors walked through the entrance door, I always enjoyed seeing the shock on their faces at the stark contrast between the grey of the outside to the abundance of colourful flowers inside. We were always very proud of our little compound, our home.

Barking dogs would serenade the guest along the short walk, unseen until given the backstage tour. The dogs eagerly waited in their kennels for the day they'd be reunited with the Western soldier who'd shown selfless compassion to do what was needed for an innocent animal that just wanted human companionship and something to eat.

–

"Afghans hate dogs, right?" was a question I was asked a lot when giving talks to schools and social groups back home in

England. It took me a while, but I finally figured out it was mostly due to the questioner not knowing any people who were practising Muslims. It's a common misconception. It is quite a simple equation really. Just find 100 people in the West, regardless of their religious beliefs, and survey them to reveal who likes dogs and who does not.

You would probably get a fifty/fifty split, give or take.

In Afghanistan it was the same outcome mostly, unless you were from a predominantly uneducated sector of society that only received religious teachings. Half of the local community had no issues with dogs and the other half feared them but did not necessarily dislike them.

The fear of dogs in Afghanistan is down to one reason and one reason only: "crazy dog's disease" or as we would know it, rabies.

If someone is bitten by a dog with rabies, unless they're pre-vaccinated or receive a vaccination within twenty-four hours, the outlook is beyond poor. 99% of those bitten will die once clinical signs show themselves.

During the time I worked and lived in Afghanistan, sadly I only ever discovered one hospital in the whole country that provided any preventative and therefore potentially life-saving vaccinations for children. So a young child en route to school coming across a stray dog snarling and aggressive in the street, well, you can imagine the terror they'd experience.

Our charity prided itself on our rabies-prevention work. School visits by our team, which included being accompanied by one of our 'bomb-proof' canine staff members, delivered an hour-long lesson to educate the youngsters on how to avoid a dog bite and, most importantly, what to do if they were bitten. As the dog was walked to the front of the class, the children nearest the aisle would shy away and hushed comments were commonplace whilst the dog ignored the overreaction of his audience. Tail wagging and excited by the cuddles he knew were coming his way, even if the children had yet to realise they wanted to give them, the dog knew he would win over the class. They always did.

Standing proudly at the front of the class wearing his or her blue scrubs with their name and veterinarian qualification noted brightly on their front left lapel, the lead vet for school that day would say "Bishi" – Dari for "sit".

As if by magic, the dog would duly sit, obediently looking up at the familiar face. The resulting gasp from the children – and even some of the teachers – was adorable.

"How can a dog understand us?", "The dog speaks Dari?" Their faces would be awash with wanting to understand what they had just witnessed. Their softly spoken questions were so endearing. A moment of pure innocence buried in discovery.

By the end of the lesson the dog would truly be in its element. The children would queue up to give it a hug or just watch in awe as the dog demonstrated its latest trick, sitting swiftly and presenting its paw for a shake. With eyes wide and big smiles, the children were transported away to a new world of discovery. Asking the dog to sit or letting it gently nibble a treat from their hands was totally unknown to them all.

But the point of the lesson was that they left fully armed with the knowledge to hopefully prevent an attack by a stray dog and, as we explained much to their delight, they were now ambassadors for Nowzad. Their mission: to teach their siblings and relatives about the dangers of rabies and show off their Nowzad animal ambassador certificate at the same time.

Across Kabul, we spent hours pasting posters to telegraph poles and compound walls that depicted the cause of rabies and how to avoid becoming a casualty. The posters were designed as cartoons, as most adult Afghans were unable to read or write.

We didn't just rescue dogs and cats, treat strays, and help to prevent the spread of disease. We also educated and trained the community, both young and old, so that people and animals could live together better. Together, we were making a positive difference for both the people *and* the animals. And I was super proud of that.

I loved my job. I loved living and working in Afghanistan. This charity was my dream. My life. And the icing on the cake was that my wife had chosen to work in Afghanistan as well, although not for Nowzad. I had to admit I was one lucky guy.

Kaisa, my Norwegian wife, was the best thing that had ever happened to me. A seriously qualified mountaineering instructor, athletic, tall and blonde, she had a fierce reputation for getting the job done, holding herself amongst the best of them. She had travelled independently to Afghanistan before we had met, on her way to work for an organisation to improve the lives of young Afghan girls. Kaisa was their country manager.

We had met over a cup of tea and our shared passion for climbing. Being in her company inspired me to achieve more. We never let a single day go to waste. Our time together was always full of laughter and love.

The young girls that Kaisa worked with in Afghanistan had arranged a traditional Afghan ceremony for us when we had returned from our actual wedding in the mountains of the western US. They loaned us the colourful time-honoured costumes that a bride and her groom were expected to wear. Standing in my long baggy shalwar kameez with a fancy waist-coat, I'd been mesmerised by Kaisa's stunning beauty as she twirled and danced in her bead-covered dress, her laughter infectiously spreading to girls who looked up to Kaisa and had gone out of their way to provide this experience of a lifetime.

I adored the country and most of the people. How could I not? I was doing the best job in the world with amazing staff and friends, helping to rebuild a country and its people, with the most beautiful woman at my side. Having said that, we knew that one day we would return to the West.

Our conversation would always circle back to our eventual move to Norway and our imagined rustic farmhouse, with its private road winding down through the grass pastures, nestled between the majestic Norwegian mountains overlooking the edge of a crystal-clear fjord. Kaisa's beautiful blue eyes, which I was more than happy to lose myself in, would sparkle with excitement as I enthused about what my new Norwegian life would be like. She would chuckle as I laid bare my keenness for owning my very own "stabbur", a tradition-al wooden barn commonly used for storing food during days gone by. I thought those barns just looked so cool and ours was going to be converted into our very own gym. I could not wait. Moving to Norge land and living amongst the mountains with my very own shield-maiden was my goal. That had al-ways been the default plan since the day we met, and I knew I would want for literally nothing else in the world. For the time being, we placed our dream on hold and made the most of our time in Kabul together. I was beyond in love with her.

We lived together under the same roof as Mujtaba, who

took the single room at the end of the large house so that he could be on call if the animals had an emergency during the dark hours, which often happened.

And the house was also home to an Afghan-American called Najwa. I had known her for many years before she accepted my job offer to become the country manager for the charity. She had taken the family bedroom on the top floor of the house, along with her husband Mirwais, our driver and logistics manager. Mirwais became a good friend, and like Mujtaba, would call me "Lala", the Dari word meaning "brother". Mirwais and Najwa had little Ibrahim, which proudly made me an uncle, or "kaka".

Every night at four-thirty on the dot, six days a week, Kaisa, Mirwais, Mujtaba, and I would meet up for our daily workout in the very small but adequate home gym we had assembled between us.

Cooking was a communal effort we all enjoyed unless we ordered in a pizza – Kabul offered a pretty good home delivery service – before hanging out in the evenings talking or just watching a movie together.

Life was pretty good inside our Kabul bubble. I was under no illusions that Afghanistan was an easy or safe place to live, or that our presence was wholly welcome by all. But Kabul was feeling safer, definitely more prosperous and harmonious. Sure, it was a bubble. But you have to start somewhere. And given enough time, we could have enlarged that sphere and made more people's lives better.

What we did not know was that our bubble was about to burst.

June – July 2021

We never had the benefit of Captain Hindsight. I wish we had. Looking back now, it's all much clearer which assumptions were wrong, where we were naïve, and what we didn't know.

For my own sanity and personal integrity, I would like to set the scene and correct the utter rubbish I have read on social media – and even in the mainstream media – about why and how the Taliban were able to retake Afghanistan so easily. And when I say easily, I mean so easily that without really having to engage in battle with the Afghan army, a force of poorly trained and mostly ill-equipped Taliban fighters with no air cover swept across the country in just fourteen days. No one saw that one coming.

On the 29th of February 2020 in Doha, Qatar, the United States (under the presidency of Donald Trump) and Abdul Ghani Baradar signed the Agreement for Bringing Peace to Afghanistan, more commonly known as the Doha Agreement, with the intention of bringing an end to the war in Afghanistan.

In Doha, the negotiations on behalf of the Americans were conducted by the American diplomat and foreign policy expert, Zalmay Khalilzad. The Taliban delegation was headed by Abdul Ghani Baradar and he was no insignificant player in the great Afghan game. He was, no less, a co-founder of the original Taliban.

After the 2001 terrorist attack on the United States, Abdul Ghani Baradar had been at the top of the coalition's most wanted list. That was until a deal was brokered with the Pakistani intelligence service and he was finally apprehended in 2010. The Pakistani authorities held him in detention at the request of the Americans until 2018 when his release was requested by Zalmay Khalilzad.

The wheels of fate had already started turning very slowly in the direction of the events leading to August 2021.

Abdul Ghani Baradar won the war that started many years earlier by just waiting it out.

Prime Minister Boris Johnson, standing up in the House of Commons on the 8th of July 2021, stated, "There is no military path to victory for the Taliban." It's probably the only truthful thing he ever said. The Taliban didn't need to win militarily. They needed patience.

I always remember a Taliban fighter who was interviewed many years ago, (sadly I don't recall his name or by whom the interview was made) and when asked how long it would take to win the war against the United States, the fighter said simply, "The moment Americans arrive in Afghanistan they are looking at their watches waiting for the day they can go home. A Taliban fighter does not look at the time. He is home."

Never was a truer word said in this conflict.

The US government decided that it was the only player with skin in the game. At no point in the negotiations did the United States believe it beneficial to bring to the peacemaking table the democratically elected government of Afghanistan. The peacemaking deal also included zero participation from any of the coalition partners. The deal was, without a doubt, the precursor to the collapse of the Afghan National Security Force (ANSF), and therefore the fall of Afghanistan.

The deal offered by the Americans was simple: "We are leaving. Don't shoot us in the back." The Taliban rapidly put pen to paper.

All coalition troops were to have left Afghanistan by 1ˢᵗ of May 2021. Britain, along with all coalition partners, had no choice but to follow suit. Then Joe Biden was elected president of the United States. He extended the deadline until September 11ᵗʰ 2021, the twentieth anniversary of the terrorist attack on the Twin Towers. I guessed that some analyst had rightly assumed that the Taliban would restrain from risking further confrontation with the Americans. They'd already waited and waited. Another few weeks wouldn't have made that much of a difference. After the US had left, they would have plenty of time to march across Afghanistan.

Both Trump and Biden wanted to be the one who could claim they brought America's soldiers home. Neither seemed to care about what would happen to Afghanistan in the process. As I write this book, neither have shown any further interest in a country in which 1,921 American soldiers' lives were lost as a direct result of hostile action with over 20,000 injured in a war against a force that harboured al-Qaeda. Its terrorist attack killed almost 3,000 people, injured thousands more, and caused $10 billion in damage. And yet after twenty years of Afghanistan heading in the right direction, a solid generation of change due to the ultimate sacrifice of too many soldiers, we were suddenly talking about the Taliban being able to retake Kabul.

Twenty years of struggle and loss for what?

I have listened to countless politicians from both sides of the house and from both sides of the pond attempt to spin the withdrawal as a positive outcome.

I have yet to be convinced.

Almost no Afghan Army unit engaged the advancing Taliban. Corruption was sadly rife, and the United States and its partners had failed miserably to tackle it. Funding for "ghost soldiers" was mostly paid without any form of scrutiny or oversight. And when inspections were ordered by the coalition, smartly kitted-out Afghan soldiers would parade, ready for the audit. The problem was that these same soldiers had paraded elsewhere the day before representing another unit that never actually existed either, except on some Excel spreadsheet.

No one seemed to care.

The unprecedented speed of the Taliban's provincial gains surprised US intelligence, from whom we were receiving our reports and basing our assessment of what our charity would do in the coming months. I distinctly remember being in our newly refurbished office in Kabul, the well-polished floor glaring brightly as the mid-morning sun poured in through the large open windows, as I read out the latest intelligence assessment. It was early May 2021.

"We have until October at the earliest before the Taliban will be in a position to retake Kabul."

It was just too much to comprehend. It was kind of surreal. Every day we discussed what we would do as a charity. And always we returned to the expectation that there was no way Biden would let this happen. Over the last twenty years the sacrifices had been too great. There was no way the West would just abandon Afghanistan. Surely there was a deal to be made with the Taliban. At the time of the withdrawal, the country was among the poorest in the world according to the World Bank and it relied on foreign aid.

Besides, there were still several thousand American troops stationed in Iraq even after the Iraqi government had called for a complete expulsion of all foreign troops, and Biden had announced that he would end combat missions there. They're still there. And in Syria. And every other country from which they've "pulled out". Surely a deal could and would be struck.

Right up to the last second, I truly believed that a deal would happen.

I was hardly alone. The reason why the evacuation was such a shitstorm for us was because we received zero guidance or planning from the British government, who you'd expect to have some sort of plan. Except it didn't. Let me quote the Foreign Select Committee's findings on the evacuation: "The UK Government failed effectively to shape or respond to Washington's decision to withdraw, despite having had 18 months' notice."

The US military had attempted, by all accounts, to leave several thousand troops permanently stationed in Afghanistan but the Biden administration had overruled them. As soon as that happened, the Pentagon went full throttle with withdrawing all troops from Afghanistan regardless of the tactical picture on the ground.

Reports of meetings held in the Pentagon and White House, readily available online, state that General Austin Miller (head of NATO's Resolute Support Mission in Afghanistan which included commanding all US troops on the ground, and a highly decorated combat soldier himself) recommended handing over Bagram Air Base to the Afghan military as soon as possible. General Miller believed that speed would equal safety in withdrawing all US troops from Afghanistan. He, along with many in the decision-making process, believed that US assets would be at threat of renewed Taliban attacks should they overstay their agreed timeline.

In the dead of the night on the 1st of July 2021, the US military abandoned Bagram Air Base. The Afghan commander came to work in the morning to find the US had gone. He had been given no warning of the US intention to leave.

Bagram was an old Soviet airbase and the US had made it their centre of operations for all their military activity. It contained two runways, compared to Kabul's civilian airport which contained only one runway. This rather important technical detail was often overlooked but one I thought about constantly during those following few weeks.

With Bagram Air Base gone, there would be little to no air support available should any Afghan units come under sustained and overwhelming Taliban fire. Due to the dwindling force strength on the ground (less than 1,000 by the beginning of July) as dictated by the Trump/Biden timeline for the evacuation, the military command was forced to compromise. They either had enough troops to secure the American embassy in Kabul or to keep Bagram operational during the withdrawal. Apparently, they could not maintain both.

Leaving as they did in the dead of night, the United States administration showed complete contempt for their Afghan colleagues whom they had trained, worked with, and at times fought alongside during the previous twenty years. Every Afghan I subsequently talked to felt betrayed. I felt betrayed. The sacrifices made by Marines that I had fought alongside had been in vain. No doubt about it.

Inquiry after inquiry has since been conducted into the withdrawal from Afghanistan by relevant American agencies and most have concluded reluctantly that the abandonment of Bagram Air Base led to the hastening of the collapse of Afghanistan's government and its armed forces. I would add that the military high command and staffers in the White

House demonstrated extremely poor leadership. They got the important decisions wrong.

Within days of the abandonment of Bagram Air Base, morale amongst the Afghan troops plummeted to an all-time low. They had lost their air support and military oversight. The knock-on effect was that the grunt on the ground, the common Afghan soldier, was no longer prepared to fight for a government in Kabul as it would mostly involve dying.

Yet on the 10th of August (just five days before the Taliban entered Kabul and retook the country) I heard completely the opposite to what we knew was happening. Our online meeting with the charitable intelligence organisation, which provided us and most of the other non-governmental organisations working in Afghanistan with detailed briefings on all things related to security matters, gave us our final update.

I listened intently, hastily writing notes in my notebook so I could relay the details to my Afghan team cramped together anxiously in the office on the ground floor.

The in-country station manager's slides highlighted that the planning for the withdrawal was nearly complete except for an international military presence in Kabul and Kandahar, but some categories of military and non-military personnel remained and/or were returning. The fact that some units were returning was the key indicator that somebody somewhere was not happy with how things were panning out with the drawdown of troops.

The US narrative had already begun to change, and pledges of support were being given to the Afghan Army in the form of "over the horizon" airstrikes, meaning air support from outside Afghanistan from American military bases within the Middle East. Figures showed that over 8,000 Taliban fighters had been killed or wounded during July, yet they were still managing to increase their attacks, resulting in the fact that by July 2021 they controlled over 57% of Afghanistan, which included capturing six of the provincial capitals. The Taliban's military strategy was straightforward and described by one military analyst after the evacuation as simply "smart". I completely agreed with him.

The Taliban played a blinder, as we would say in England.

They took control of all major border crossings in and out of Afghanistan, whilst controlling the main highways between the large cities. This ensured that the Afghan government was unable to resupply its army with rations, ammunition, or, most importantly, reinforcements.

The Taliban had effectively cut the head from the snake, and those Afghan army units, now cut off from their resupply chains, simply dropped their weapons and fled into the night.

Meanwhile, the slides from the charitable intelligence organisation unbelievably highlighted a potential security plan being floated by the Afghan government to recapture Afghanistan from the Taliban within six months.

"What?" I burst out laughing. Thankfully all attendees' mics were muted. As if to answer my unheard question the presenter added, "Clearly there is no further detail available on this improbable plan." I could tell it was said with some sarcasm.

I dismissed it as pure bravado from a collapsing government trying to maintain the pretence of influence. In twenty years of intense coalition support, the Afghan government had not truly controlled Afghanistan. And with the Americans almost gone, they were genuinely talking about being able to recapture the whole country within six months?

"Not a hope in hell," I said to no one.

Contrast the foolish optimism of the outgoing Afghan government with the nonchalance of the British. The Foreign Secretary at the time, Dominic Raab, the minister charged with the responsibility of the United Kingdom's interests overseas, stayed on holiday whilst the evacuation took place. He refused to fly home to personally deal with the situation.

Later, the Foreign Select Committee examining the evacuation would state, "The fact that the department's top civil servant did not return until the civilian evacuation was over... is difficult to understand and impossible to excuse."

According to The Guardian (Friday 13th of August 2021, article by Patrick Wintour, Peter Beaumont and Julian Berger), there were as many as 200 British diplomats and soldiers to be evacuated, not to mention all Afghan staff who had been associated with the British military during the past twenty years. This has been estimated to be as many as 4,000 people. They included civil servants, judges, soldiers, feminists, journalists, and aid workers. The reasonable assumption was that anyone British or associated with anyone or anything Western would be held hostage, or worse, killed. And yet it was not deemed worthy of an interrupted vacation.

The UK government flew over 1,000 British service men and women, from 16 Air Assault Brigade, to Afghanistan on August 17th to support the US military who were now holding Kabul's airport since it was surrounded by Taliban fighters. In an audio recording on the Imperial War Museum's website, Lieutenant Colonel David Middleton said that the "security of the airfield was not assumed" and that the American Marines had a "difficult task" with perimeter security. It did not take the brains of an archbishop to realise a clusterfuck was unfolding.

The world had not seen an operation attempted like this since the fall of Saigon on the 30th of April 1975.

But the chump stayed on holiday. To this day I cannot fathom that.

And that is where we found ourselves, in a country now abandoned by the very people who once promoted its salvation.

We had given young Afghans, the true heirs to their country, choices. And they were choosing education, the oversubscribed university courses were testimony to that. Afghanistan now had female judges and even a few of the provinces had female governors. At Nowzad, we employed the first-ever female Afghan veterinarians. After twenty years, progress and cultural change was slowly happening.

I still find it so hard to grasp. So many gave up their lives in the fight to finally bring peace to Afghanistan and allow a democratically elected government to lead the country. I had personally carried the coffin of one of my Marines who had made the ultimate sacrifice for the people of Afghanistan. Twenty years of the ultimate sacrifice by our courageous soldiers, sailors, and aviators, plus nearly three trillion dollars in aid and defence spending during the tenure of four presidents of the United States culminated in the Taliban regime being replaced with the Taliban regime.

You could not make that up. Ever.

11 August 2021

The glowing embers drifted up on the thermals from the heat of the intensely burning fire. Fifteen years of Nowzad's animal welfare history were riding the hot winds to oblivion.

I stood, my Yeti mug in hand, but I had not sipped any of the hot tea it held. Instead, I just watched, mesmerised, as the ashes of our commitment to animal welfare here floated skyward.

Basir, currently stood down from his kennel-cleaning duties, was positioned amongst piles of A4 paper torn from plastic files now in a heap to one side. As the roaring flames began to die down, he'd scoop up another armful of irreplaceable archives on what we had achieved in Afghanistan and feed the insatiable belly of the fire until it blazed high once more.

I felt numb. I could not process the fact that everything we had worked for was now being reduced to ashes. We had contracts with a myriad of embassies and military bases, usually written but occasionally verbal, to look after their dogs. They were used to keep their entry checkpoints safe. We vaccinated their animals, spayed them, and cared for them when they were sick. These documents and those of the nearly 1,700 soldier companion animal rescues were, right in front of my eyes, being consigned to a fiery end.

But I knew that when the Taliban took over, these records were also potentially very damaging. We had no idea how the Taliban would react. We worked with and for Western governments, which were supporting the Afghan government that was in the process of being overthrown. By the 11th of August it was as clear as day that there was no stopping the advance of the Taliban. The staff were, quite rightly, frantic with concern at how they would be treated by the incoming Taliban fighters, especially due to the nature of our animal welfare work which included supporting the Western forces.

In that moment I hated both Trump and Biden with a passion that I knew would never die out. An old man (either one, take your pick) who, in my opinion, was well past his prime to be leading a country, had thrown to the wind everything that had been achieved by so many organisations attempting to make a difference in Afghanistan. As a team of Western and Afghan allies alike, we had toiled so hard for the monumental gains in animal welfare and increased opportunities for women. And yet with a stroke of the pen, it was going to be wiped out in a matter of days.

And so we bit the bullet and destroyed all evidence that tied us to former soldier animal rescues, working dogs' vaccinations and treatment, import and export paperwork, and customs clearance for working dogs that operated in Afghanistan.

Deep down, we had all hoped beyond hope that the Americans and the coalition would change their decision to abandon Afghanistan. But they hadn't. So here we were, just five weeks later, handing the Taliban the keys to Kabul.

I called a meeting of the entire staff because of a taxi that had arrived earlier that morning. It had come from the British embassy, one of those we had a verbal agreement with. The taxi contained the last of the embassy cats that had once roamed the grounds of the secure compound. Fed and cared for by the staff while offering normality and comfort in return, they were a welcome distraction for those separated from loved ones back in the UK during their tour of duty. As with the dogs, Nowzad provided vital vaccinations and neutering to the cat population. It was always a pleasure to visit the embassy garden and watch the staff play with the newest puppies we had brought in for a play date. The staff and puppies alike enjoyed the all-important positive interaction.

But for me, it was the handwritten note attached to one of the travel crates containing a cat. It simply read, "We are abandoning the embassy – please take care of the cats."

In a sign of the British government's complete incompetence to plan for the evacuation, the embassy was abandoned with just nine hours' notice. The staff were unprepared and untested for what to do in such a situation. The embassy closed, and the Foreign Commonwealth Development Office embassy staff were flown to Dubai where, it was deemed, they could manage the evacuation processes. Yet it was soon clear that to facilitate the evacuation of thousands of eligible Afghans, they needed to be on the ground in person, in Kabul. So on the 17th of August, a replacement embassy team was flown back to Kabul airport to assist with the evacuation.

Shockingly, it was later discovered that sensitive documents, such as details of Afghans who had worked for the British government and therefore most likely including Nowzad vets cleared to enter the embassy, had not been removed or destroyed. That information would now most likely fall into the hands of the Taliban.

I sat on a wooden hardbacked chair I had borrowed from our dining area, facing the collective staff with our office manager, Farid. He'd been tasked with keeping our twenty-four-strong team in check. He and Mujtaba sat side by side on the three-person off-white leather sofa. Najwa was swallowed up by the huge plush matching armchair that was positioned directly opposite them. Hamida and Zahra, two of our young female vets, perched on either side of her atop the huge arms of the chair. Basir, Reshad, Juma, Mobin, Malalai, Fazad, our other Zahra, Zakia, Qais e Gul, Salim, Merwais, and Amanullah all crammed in where space allowed. The layout was dictated by the odd-shaped 'L' corner of the room that we had designated as our meeting area. It was not designed for this many people. The rest of the team were at the donkey shelter and would be given a call as soon as this meeting had finished.

Normally our meetings were positive and can-do, discussing the animal welfare cases of the day and who was going to be tasked with what. Farid would announce which young vet would be delivering the medical presentation of the day, an initiative he had added to the clinic routine to assist with improving the team's knowledge and their English language skills.

But today the mood was sombre and as real as it gets.

As I surveyed the room, I realised everyone was looking to me for direction. I felt the weight of the responsibility. They all knew that most of the Westerners living and working in Kabul were booking last-minute flights to leave. Currently, the price of a ticket had nearly trebled. I guess they were expecting me to say I was leaving. Certainly Kaisa and I could have. We had the passports. We had enough money. We could pack a simple bag and scoot.

But that was never an option. Or to be more accurate, I was not running off with my tail between my legs for safety while my staff at Nowzad were left holding the bag.

I looked around at the gathered faces. Hamida's infectious smile and eyes wide with enthusiasm for her work were always the first thing you noticed as she walked into a room. She had never known rule under the Taliban. She was five when the United States had forcibly removed the Taliban from their vice-like grip on Afghanistan. She grew up attending school and eventually deciding her own career path with the full support of her family. And just like Malalai had done before her, she would in time decide who she wanted to marry.

But now her smile was gone. Instead a look of dread was all I could see. She now faced a grim future where she would be married off to somebody she had never met, to care for children she'd be forced to bear. Her life would strictly revolve around the kitchen. The life we had inspired her to seek out would be gone.

I knew I couldn't just walk away from Hamida, nor the others. The notion of boarding a flight and leaving the team and our animals to a fate unknown was unthinkable.

I had a vague notion of a plan that I had briefly discussed with the charity's trustees. There was no meat to the bones as they say, and I had yet to realise what a beast I was about to create.

Only Najwa knew what I was going to say, and she had not been happy with part of my decision, the bit I knew was needed to make it work. But as I told her, I was the boss. My decision would stand.

I did not bother with any pleasantries, I just nodded in the direction of everyone and then began. "I am staying in Kabul, and I am going to try and have you evacuated to the United Kingdom. Those who would prefer to stay and ride it out as the Taliban retake Afghanistan, please let Najwa know."

As Najwa finished translating, the room erupted into a

hundred shouted questions as everybody attempted to process what I had just said.

I couldn't really answer most of the questions. I couldn't promise they would be evacuated, but I didn't see why they shouldn't be and I was going to do everything I could to make it a reality. They fulfilled the guidelines of vulnerable Afghans. They hadn't worked directly for the British government but they had worked for a British-run charity, the British embassy, and Western military bases. I knew that if I stayed, in effect behind enemy lines during the evacuation, I would attract the attention of the world's media. Media could not land a plane. Used correctly however, the media could be used to convince the government to land a plane. It substantially heightened my own chance of being held hostage as a former Royal Marine and as someone supporting the outgoing Afghan government. But it was a risk I had to take.

Mujtaba asked the inevitable question, "What about the animals? The dogs and cats in our care?"

I smiled at him. "We are taking them with us."

He just looked at me, bewilderment etched across his face. But he knew better than to ask how. Which was good, as I had no freaking idea how we were going to pull it off. And I had yet to inform Jen, our adoptions manager, of the headache about to come her way. Importing a dog or cat from a developing-world country is no easy administrative task when you have months to prepare, let alone just a few days.

Our plan was straightforward: we would raise the funds to charter our own aircraft. I was sure that our staff would be deemed eligible for evacuation as vulnerable Afghans. Because they were. We would fly them out in the passenger cabin and the animals in cargo.

From the very beginning we had no intention of using military aircraft or personnel. We only needed visas and permission to land an aircraft.

Straightforward. Yes, it was administratively complex. And expensive. But these were hurdles we could overcome.

13 August 2021

On the 13th of August, the United Kingdom announced that Operation Pitting, the military code word for their evacuation efforts, would begin in a few days.

British nationals, Afghans who had worked for the British government, and vulnerable Afghans would be prioritised for evacuation.

We all believed it. We believed that once the government knew about us, it would evacuate us. Our staff worked with military units, cared for military dogs. We believed they had every right to be evacuated alongside interpreters.

On the same day, we officially launched Operation Ark when I was interviewed on the one-and-only Phil Lassman's "#DoggyPeople" show. The day before, the Taliban had taken the second and third largest cities. Kabul was effectively isolated. I was working the media to bring attention to Nowzad and the situation in Afghanistan.

While I talked about our female staff and what the future would hold for them, I could not sit still. I wandered randomly around the upstairs of the house as I chatted to Phil over my phone. My emotions, already bubbling beneath the surface, now threatened to erupt as I tried to convey the seriousness of what we were about to face. I struggled to keep it together to be honest.

When asked what would happen to the charity and to the animals we cared for as the Taliban retook Afghanistan, I had no answer. I choked up. I knew it meant either releasing them or putting them to sleep. There was no alternative.

It was a perfect storm. The Covid pandemic had previously grounded all international flights and the day they restarted flying, the Centre for Disease Control in America had implemented a ban on dogs from Afghanistan being allowed to enter, even if they were vaccinated. We now had a backlog of dogs waiting for their new homes. Some were soldier-companion animal rescues whilst others had been rescued from the streets and had reliable forever homes found for them.

I could not just abandon them all. It was unthinkable.

On the spot I made up the now infamous name of Operation Ark when Phil asked me what we were going to call our fundraising campaign. To me it was simple. Not that I'm religious, but I'd read the Bible when I was a kid. Noah building a wooden Ark for the animals and his extended family was what we needed right now. The Taliban was flooding across Afghanistan, and we needed to ride out the approaching storm. The chartered aircraft would be our Ark.

Nowzad patron Peter Egan reposted the interview with Phil on his social media channels. Our desperate mission went viral. Operation Ark became a juggernaut that wasn't about to slow down for anyone.

The next few days became a whirlwind of interviews with the world's press and online meetings. My name began to trend on social media.

To emphasise the horrors about to befall Afghan women, and especially the seven who worked for Nowzad, Hamida volunteered to be interviewed by the media. She became our voice for Afghan women.

I was blown away by her conviction to tell the truth. And it worried me intensely that she was putting herself in the firing line of the incoming Taliban. If I failed to get her out, she would be forced into hiding. She did not hold back from being critical of the Taliban leadership.

Whilst Hamida and I were doing what I thought was a sterling effort in representing our need to be evacuated across the world's media, I needed a dog who could tug at the heart-strings and happily appear in interviews to help us fundraise for the aircraft. My dog, Ragnar, was just too damn big and boisterous.

What I needed was an Ewok.

Ewok had been a resident with us since May 2021, but prior to that he had been on the Nowzad books as Alex, his owner having brought him in for the free rabies vaccine updates and health checks that we offered all Afghan nationals.

Little Alex was a pure-bred Pomeranian from a breeder in Russia. It's still something I struggle to get my head around, but there was a thriving market for pure-breds in Afghanistan. Obviously since we were in the rabies-prevention game, we weren't going to turn down the opportunity to vaccinate a dog annually regardless of whether it was a rescue or not.

Much to the surprise of all of us, Dr Mujtaba had received a call from Alex's Afghan owner who bluntly gave Mujtaba a choice: we either take Alex in as a rescue or he was going to be ditched on the streets. Now a proud owner of an American visa, Alex's owner was leaving Afghanistan due to the impending turmoil from the US withdrawal. We would have helped him transport Alex to America had he asked but he had no interest in taking his dog with him.

"Dickhead!" was my unprofessional outburst at the news from Mujtaba.

I had no need to ask Mujtaba how he had answered. Little Alex wouldn't last more than a few days on the unforgiving streets of Kabul. "When is he bringing the dog in?"

"He dropped him off a few minutes ago. Zahra the Second

is giving him a physical check-up now," Mujtaba replied smiling. He had a big smile. I smiled back.

"I had better go and say hello then." I turned and walked out from the clinic, leaving Mujtaba to carry on with the vaccine prep he was in the middle of when I had originally barged in.

Dr Zahra was known as "Dr Zahra the Second" for a very practical reason – we already had a Dr Zahra who had been with us for nearly a year. Dr Zahra the Second had only just finished her time as an intern at Nowzad, but throughout had impressed us with her veterinary aptitude. We'd immediately offered her a role as an assistant vet, which she was only too happy to accept.

As I entered the room, she was already weighing the little man. Her jet-black hair was tucked away under her light purple headscarf and her Nowzad-embroidered blue scrubs looked fresh on. As per the cultural expectations in this part of the world, she wore long sleeves down to her wrists. Currently little Alex was being very gently poked and prodded by her blue latex glove-covered hands. She looked up and smiled. Her piercing brown eyes radiated enthusiasm for what she was doing and that made me smile immediately.

The enthusiasm of our whole team for animal welfare was music to my ears. I couldn't have asked for a more in-tune group of employees who placed animal welfare as their chief priority.

"Hello, Sir, how are you?" she said. I had given up trying to convince everyone to drop the Sir. It was a battle I had no chance of winning.

Still grinning, I replied, "Khoob, tashakor" (Good, thank you). My feeble attempt to respond in kind never seemed to do justice to the fluent English that most of the vet team spoke.

I was stunned. The brown long-haired bundle of cuteness stared at me from his sitting position in the aluminium scale. "How could somebody just abandon this little guy?"

Dr Zahra returned to her work and concentrated on making her clinical notes about the underweight Pomeranian. All our vets were expected to make their notes in English so I figured I had probably put her under some slight pressure as the boss had just gatecrashed her physical check-up of the new resident.

I extended my hands to scoop up the little fluff ball. I looked over at the notes. His age had been noted at around nine years old. Yet he looked way smaller than any Pomeranian I had ever seen. I guessed it was due to some unscrupulous breeder who had ripped him from his puppy-mill mum far too early and then failed to feed him what he needed during those important early years.

I studied his hair-covered face, his black wet nose, and deep black eyes. He was covered with long whispery brown hair. He was staring directly at me as I held him aloft.

"You, my little friend, are not an Alex," I told him with authority. "You are an Ewok. And like the original Ewoks, you are part of the solution." Alex, now Ewok, showed no emotion in this sudden change of name.

"Dr Zahra, please change his name to Ewok, E-W-O-K, thank you."

She looked at me, confused. "Ewok?"

I laughed. "Yes, he is now an Ewok," I confirmed. "When we get back to the office, I will show you what an Ewok is."

Now I was sitting with Ewok in my arms on the exercise

bike in my small self-contained gym set-up. My legs rode the pedals round as I went nowhere. Having just told the staff I was going to evacuate them to England I needed to think. Exercising helped me do that.

Ewok's face was almost lost in the abundance of whispery hair that protruded from every part of his body. He sure did look like an Ewok. And he was the perfect amount of cuteness to capture supporters' imaginations.

There was no way on this planet I was just going to abandon him, let alone the staff.

15 August 2021

We sat as one large group, ignoring the unrelenting heat. Every now and then a phone would ping and a member of the team would blurt out an update from a family member from the many Messenger groups we all belonged to. Farid was co-ordinating it all, double-checking sources. Together we were drawing a picture of events as they happened on the ground. Hamida and Zahra sat, hands folded and resting on their laps, their faces etched with worry, mirroring our own. I sat with my Yeti mug, once more full of hot tea that I had yet to drink.

Every now and again I would look anxiously at Kaisa who was sitting with me on the two-person sofa. I watched her face as she stared, transfixed by every word Mujtaba or Farid said. It dawned on me that Mujtaba and Farid were both listening to and reading reports in Dari that they then translated into English, which Kaisa in turn would translate in her head into Norwegian.

Najwa had stood up to take a call. She returned to our group, her face completely expressionless.

"That was Safi," she said slowly. Safi was one of three staff members who worked the day shift at our actual dog shelter. Currently we had over 140 dogs in residence.

Our dog shelter was on the southern edge of Kabul city, near a village called Gul Bagh. We had located the shelter there for an obvious reason. Caring for that many dogs here in a popular residential area would not have gone down well with the locals. The noise from all that barking would have been deafening. Karte Se, our neighbourhood, was an affluent area and a simple phone call to the right person would have seen us shut down.

"A Taliban convoy just drove past. Safi said there were hundreds of them." Everybody in the room was silent and staring into space.

The dog shelter was just a twenty-minute drive from where we were sat.

Hamida burst into tears and fled the room. Kaisa immediately stood up and followed her out to offer what comfort she could.

"Oh shit," I said to nobody. Najwa just nodded back at me before adding, "The guys will stay at the shelter tonight. They don't want to travel back into Kabul today."

We had placed a portacabin on site. It contained bunk beds, a fridge, and small gas cooker. I concurred with their assessment of attempting to travel on the roads today which were choked with Taliban fighters converging on the capital.

The office was airless and felt restrictive. I stood. I focused my attention on Najwa and Farid. "Rally the troops and let's go round the compound one last time," I directed. "Ensure we have burnt everything that connects us to anything to do with America."

Our office shelves were empty already. File folders that once contained the details of every rescue, surgery, or contract we'd had with Western companies and embassies, had already been burnt. But with the Taliban about to drive along our street it seemed to be a pretty good idea to make sure we had indeed destroyed everything that could connect us.

Muhammad Nasir Haqqani, a Taliban commander, approached the gates of Kabul with his incredibly well-armed men on the 15th of August. They were held at the gates by the higher Taliban command. The Taliban war council did not want Kabul and its population to be in the middle of a bloody battle between them and Afghan governments forces. They had seen the bloody civil war between Massoud and Hekmatyar in the early 90s that had flattened Kabul and left thousands of dead. They had no wish to repeat that horror.

In a news article that appeared later, Muhammad Nasir Haqqani was interviewed and voiced his clear surprise that when they arrived on the outskirts of Kabul, fired up with adrenaline and excitement at the prospect of finally retaking Kabul, fully prepared for the heavy fighting that would likely ensue as they stormed the capital, they found no Afghan military or police units waiting for them.

In fact, there was no resistance at all. The police had discarded their uniforms, abandoned their posts, and blended swiftly into the local population. When Taliban fighters were eventually given permission by their leadership to enter Kabul, they claimed control of the city once more without firing a shot within the capital.

I found Najwa by the improvised burn pit. She was silently watching the flames dance wildly around a burning rectangle of solid wood.

I realised instantly what was slowly being engulfed by flames. "Where was that?" I asked numbly. The handmade wooden plaque of solid oak contained an engraved American flag. 'Nowzad' was engraved around the stars and stripes. It had been gifted to our clinic by an American soldier celebrating being reunited with his much-loved four-legged companion. North Carolina had been the dog's destination where the playful hound once more stood at the side of his grateful soldier. The plaque was a beautiful piece of work, hand-carved by the soldier himself. Destroying it was heartbreaking, but

I knew attempting to hide it in the compound wasn't worth the risk.

"Still on the wall," she replied solemnly and with just a hint of sarcasm.

Just how the hell had we missed that? It was in my eyeline every time I entered the main office from the outer door. "Bloody hell," I said, shaking my head in disbelief.

"You ok?" I asked Najwa as we both stared into the hypnotic flames carrying out their task with ruthless efficiency. I knew it was a stupid question.

"No, not really." She paused before continuing, "What is going to happen to my Afghanistan?"

I had no answer for her. Najwa had sacrificed so much to come back to Kabul as a twenty-year-old woman. Her family had escaped with her to America when she was just two years old as the Russians invaded Afghanistan. Najwa could have opted to build a career in the Land of Opportunity. Instead, after gaining an education, she chose to return as the American and coalition forces supposedly freed the country from the oppressiveness of the Taliban regime, aiming to help rebuild Afghanistan.

Now in this moment, nobody except the Taliban themselves knew what was coming next for a country that, for a brief period, had experienced so much positive change. I had no words of comfort to offer. What could I have said? I was in as much shock as she was with how the world had just abandoned Afghanistan. We stood in silence, each lost in our own thoughts as the plaque slowly turned to ash.

Mujtaba looked up and called us over. We both sat, Najwa in her own chair and I perched on the arm of the sofa that was now occupied by Kaisa and Hamida, who had now exchanged her blue clinic scrubs for a long all-covering black outfit and thick black headscarf. She was taking no chances should the Taliban come calling.

I squeezed Kaisa's hand to reassure her everything was going to be ok. I had to be honest with myself, it was more for me. I just needed to feel she was there.

The Taliban I'd fought as a Marine were headed this way. Nobody had any idea how they would treat a former Royal Marine when they came across one.

Reports were coming in from the team's family members that the airport was attracting huge crowds of people at the main terminal entrance. The incumbent coalition forces on the ground were reporting a mass build-up of Afghans looking to flee.

Kabul airport had a single runway. It split the airport neatly into two halves. The military side was the northern area of the airfield where the coalition troops were based. Whilst visiting the north side to rescue a dog or occasionally to receive funds donated by a soldier or airman who had taken part in a fundraising event for Nowzad, I would take the opportunity to wander. There were delightful coffee and souvenir shops crammed between the hangars and admin blocks, selling finely woven Afghan carpets, trinkets and handicrafts made from jade, and mugs with "I love Kabul" printed boldly around their exterior.

I never bought any Afghan souvenirs there. The presence of the soldiers attracted "tourist" prices, which made them retail at nearly five times the price of the same item should I have purchased it out on the streets of Kabul.

The south side housed both the international and domestic civilian terminals. The crowds were mostly forming at the southern terminal road entrance. The thought crossed my mind as to how the military planned to start the evacuation itself. With thousands already crowding the gates, how would we get through? I had yet to figure that part out.

I stood up and nudged Kaisa. It was time. Reluctantly, she stood up too and we walked back to our bedroom. I opened the door for her. This was going to another painful exercise.

Opening our tall wardrobe door, we both reached into the stash cupboard which held our alcohol supplies. Westerners were only allowed to bring in one litre of spirits, but our recent trips, escorting dogs to their forever homes to be reunited happily with the soldiers who had originally rescued them, had afforded us the opportunity to build an impressive stockpile.

We walked back to the kitchen with numerous bottles balanced in our arms. The only alcohol that remained were two boxes of red wine, which I had stripped of the covering wrapper that divulged their contents. Stacked in the cupboard I figured they looked just like storage boxes and besides, I knew I would drain them soon enough in the coming days.

Glug, glug, glug was the only sound as I unhappily watched the contents of a brand-new bottle of Captain Morgan spiced rum disappear down the plug hole. Kaisa followed suit with a bottle of Tito's vodka. We both just stared into the sink as we said goodbye to the evidence. It was a hard goodbye, but I did not want to take the risk of the Taliban searching the compound and discovering our stash. If they so decided, they could dish out any punishment they saw fit, and I had no wish to be stoned to death.

When the deed was done, I took the empty bottles outside and, using a discarded house brick that had been tossed randomly into the garden, I smashed them into a million pieces before burying them in a deep hole in the garden.

On the day the Taliban came knocking on the door to Kabul, Kaisa and I, having finished emptying our alcohol stash, combined with the stress of everything going on, needed a timeout. We went to sit with our dogs, Ragnar and Cora, the latter being a super-friendly white Labrador type dog.

Way back in the February of 2020, we had been called out to rescue two young pups. Dr Reshad and I arrived at what we thought was the described location at the end of a long mud-covered track, our van wheels struggling to find purchase through the fairly deep slushy snow that lay across the track in places.

Opening the door of the van, I was hit with an icy blast of frigid air. Kabul in February was always cold and unrelenting.

Dull, rock-hard mud walls defined the rear of various dwellings and compounds, outlining the right-hand side of the road and representing the outer limit of this part of Kabul's southern suburbs. To my left a row of prickly bushes, sans leaves, guarded against the five-foot-or-so drop down the embankment. Beyond were countless ploughed fields, most likely used to grow wheat, barley, or corn but currently coated in a crisp layer of fresh snow. The gusting wind was streaking over the freshly deposited snow in unimpeded waves to deposit mini snowdrifts against the embankment beneath me.

We had been told by the caring Afghan who had rung the clinic hotline that the pups had been on their own for a day or so.

As I glanced down along the edge of the lower field closest to me, I noted that the smooth layer of snow was broken by hundreds of indents of boot-shaped muddy footprints.

I soon found out why as I slid down the short embankment, my boots and socks instantly wet as they landed in a pool of melted snow on the surface of the field proper. The bottom of the embankment, hidden from view by bushes protruding from the upper edge of the track above, was being used as a temporary toilet and it was immediately apparent upon closer inspection that it was not just snow-water I was standing in.

"Yuck." I winced as I looked around for some solid snow to stand on. Random piles of human poop stared up at me from mounds of snow that had been deposited. For me this would not have been the best place to bare your arse to the elements as the wind chill picked up. But when you consider most houses this far out from central Kabul probably had no running water or a functioning toilet, there actually weren't many options available to those living here.

My socks were wet. Nothing I could do now. I turned right to look further along the area I had scouted from above, and forged on through the minefield of shit, easily avoiding the many solid-looking piles but unable to avoid the contaminated water that flowed freely around them.

And then I spotted them. Two instantly obvious brown-coloured fur balls snuggled tight together against the bright white of the small snow hollow they occupied. They were both shivering profusely against the oncoming wind that had picked up even during the short amount of time we had been on the scene.

I called to Dr Reshad as he immediately slid down the snow-covered embankment. Sounding annoyed, he said something to the wind in Dari, which I didn't understand but figured it had something to do with the ice-cold water now saturating his footwear. I had forgotten to warn him.

Together we collected up the pups, one a light tan colour and the other a darker brown verging on black.

"You're both safe now." I guessed it was the first time they had ever been spoken to as I opened my jacket and placed the shivering tan-coloured mess into the warmth created by my body heat. Instantly I felt his wet fur coat soaking through my inner layer. It was a cold discomfort I was happy to endure. I did up my zip and kept my right hand in the main side pocket of the jacket to hold the tiny little life in place. Dr Reshad did the same with the darker pup. Carefully shielding our charges we struggled our way back up the embankment to the van.

"Think we had better wash everything when we get back to the clinic," I said, all matter-of-fact, to Dr Reshad.

He just looked at me curiously. "Why?" he asked.

"Because where we were just stood and where these pups have been crawling around is being used as a toilet..." I explained to the good doctor as he opened the van door. I pointed to his shoes. "That is not mud."

The look of horror on his face was priceless.

As we arrived back at the clinic, cold, wet, and rather smelly, I was greeted by my beautiful wife, her smile instantly warming me. She had immediately wanted to hold the light tan-coloured pup, his tiny body still shivering from the cold. I knew there and then this furball had found a place in the shield-maiden's heart, being born of snow and ice, the same as she had been in the depths of a northern Norway's harsh winter months. He was given his name, Ragnar Lothbrok. Never has a name suited a dog more.

As we entered their run together, both dogs went affectionately nuts, excitedly wagging their tails and doing their best to get as close to our faces as they could. "Down, buddy," I called out as I pushed Ragnar back down until I could close the gate behind me.

Kaisa sat down on the dusty ground and Ragnar immediately clambered into her lap. He weighed nearly twenty kilos now and was no longer a lapdog. The dogs were oblivious to the human-made madness that was building all around us. And for five minutes we forgot all about it too.

News broke later during the morning that Ashraf Ghani, the president of Afghanistan, had fled Kabul to the safety of the United Arab Emirates. He declared he had done so to avoid further bloodshed. Rumours were awash that the aircraft he used to flee the country was also carrying money that he had stolen from the Afghan treasury – $169 million according to a former ambassador to neighbouring Tajikistan, Zahir Aghbar.

Who really knows? The Taliban were here. I cared little to what Ashraf Ghani had taken with him. It had no bearing on what was happening here and now. It was obvious he was going to flee, and the only surprising thing was that he had not done so sooner.

A week or so later, towards the end of the evacuation, Ghani would issue a statement from the security of his accommodation in the UAE, apologising to the people of Afghanistan for leaving and reiterating that he never stole money from the country. I really don't think too many people cared by then. His time in power was over and the Taliban were already forming a new government.

The Taliban reneged on their promise. Not a single woman was considered for any of the key governmental posts.

Disappointment and despair did not even come close to describing how we felt.

Part 3:
Escape from Kabul

16 August 2021

Kabul airport was overrun. The scenes being beamed around the world were truly shocking. Afghans desperate to flee the advance of the Taliban had stormed the airport in the vague hope that they would be able to board one of the many commercial aircraft currently parked on the tarmac.

If you have seen the scenes from "World War Z" starring Brad Pitt, when the zombie hordes swarm over the airport in Tel Aviv, then you aren't far from knowing what it was like on the runway of the capital's airport. I am deadly serious.

People swarmed over any aircraft they could access, including a United States C-17 that was taxiing for take-off. Two Afghan lads, who had naively clung to the undercarriage as it took off, fell to their deaths, live on television.

It was horrific.

Coalition troops using armoured vehicles attempted to push those fleeing back to the terminal, but it was a losing battle. All commercial aircraft were grounded, the main carriers from Turkey, India, Pakistan, and Dubai cancelling all their flights to and from Afghanistan with immediate effect.

Both Najwa, who was thirty-four-weeks pregnant, and Kaisa had been due to fly out in the middle of the following week with Emirates. Now that was impossible.

It took nearly twenty-four hours before the thousands who had gathered could be pushed back beyond the airport terminal and for the United States to claim control of airport operations.

The mood in the Nowzad house was solemn. As the staff went about their daily business, they acknowledged each other but were clearly in a state of shock. I offered that if anyone felt like they needed to stay at home with their families they should do so. Everyone came to work.

Hamida had arrived to work distressed and crying. She had been stopped at numerous Taliban checkpoints along her journey in. Each time she was questioned where she, a woman travelling on her own, was headed.

The Taliban now roaming Kabul were from the provinces. Most only spoke Pashtu, not Dari which is the main language spoken in the capital. They believed women should conduct their lives according to the strict views enforced in the remote areas of Afghanistan where the Taliban fighters had been raised. There is a compelling video on YouTube of Taliban fighters exploring a park in the capital as they arrived victorious on the 15th of August. They have no idea what to do with the swings and merry-go-round. They had never had a childhood, raised instead on an upbringing of strict fanatical Islam.

Hamida had lied to the Talibs who questioned her. She told them she was a doctor and had urgent surgery to attend. She was too scared to tell them she was a veterinarian, for fear of being ridiculed and ordered to go home.

We offered the house to all who wished to stay at night – strength in numbers. Hamida chose to stay.

The Taliban had no uniform dress code. And that was a problem as telling who was now Talib and who just dressed like them was impossible. Reports were coming in of multiple instances where armed men would raid a house, stealing cash and valuables whilst claiming to be members of the Taliban. They weren't. But we were taking no chances.

I hastily devised a policy should the Taliban decide to come visit our compound. The debate had been lively. Most felt I should hide as soon as we knew it was Talibs at our front gate. We had already posted signage through the house dictating which rooms were women only. But I was concerned about those who weren't actually Taliban knocking at our door. I now always carried my pistol.

The plan was simple. I was to be the first to greet them at the compound gate. I would explain with Farid translating that this was an NGO and invite them in for chai (tea). Kill them with kindness.

We knew that we still needed to keep the dog shelter in the outskirts supplied, and that meant a physical visit. Mirwais and Mujtaba volunteered. They were stopped at an impromptu Taliban checkpoint along the familiar road, just a few hundred yards from the shelter itself.

It was now manned by our former baker, who had provided bread every day for the shelter. He had thrown his lot in with the Taliban. And he was more than vocal in his attempts to convince Mirwais and Mujtaba to do the same.

They had their decision to make (although I was pretty sure which way they were going to jump) and we had ours. It was a big decision – one that will haunt me for the rest of my life.

–

I stared at the Excel spreadsheet currently displayed in the open window on my laptop screen.

It was just a spreadsheet, a simple application that processes facts and figures into a manageable outcome. Just another spreadsheet amongst all the millions that had been created since the advent of computing.

But this one sucked in a way that I cannot describe.

The pang of inevitability gnawed away inside me. The otherwise seemingly boring set of numbers told an ugly truth that I did not have the stomach to confront. But there was no option but to confront it and confront it head-on.

My carefully crafted spreadsheet dictated which animals lived and which would be put to sleep or released. I screwed my eyes shut and willed with everything I had for the information it displayed to change for the better.

I opened my tired eyes. The numbers remained unchanged. But I had known that was going to happen.

"Fuck it," I said out loud to an unresponsive Ewok who was spreadeagled, asleep on the unvacuumed brown carpet floor. Unsurprisingly, our daily cleaning routine had fallen by the wayside. A fine layer of dust had begun to coat every available surface.

I closed the laptop screen with a thud.

Operation Ark's fundraising campaign had started well. So far we'd received donations from at least eighty different countries around the world and we were well on the way to receiving the money needed to charter an aircraft. This meant that our chartered aircraft would be funded purely through voluntary donations and wouldn't use any government resources, which could then go towards saving others. I had hope.

But the one thing that would not change was the number of crates we currently held in storage. I asked for an audit of all the available travel crates we had. It had taken over a day and a half to complete. Most were still flat-packed from their original journey from Dubai prior to Covid. They needed to be assembled and checked for air-worthiness. Crates we had already assembled were checked for damage and if any were found, we had to determine if we had any spare parts that could make them whole again.

And just when the staff were happy that they'd found 102 crates, I asked them to evaluate how many dogs of which size they could match to which crates. It was a complicated spreadsheet. We spent many hours rehashing and reworking the permutations of which dogs and cats would fit where.

But whichever way we looked at it, we only had 102 crates. We had 217 dogs and cats.

We could not take them all.

We needed to decide who was carried to forever homes in the West, who was released to take their chances on the streets, and which ones would be put to sleep. I had to call it.

We were going to save 171 animals in 102 air-worthy travel crates. Fourteen dogs, who were never going to be suitable for rehoming, would be released; they had a chance to survive as they had once done. Thirty-two dogs who were older than twelve would humanely be put to sleep. All the dogs that were eligible to be evacuated with us were brought to the clinic. It was a tight fit but we managed it.

After nearly ten years of operating, the Nowzad dog shelter closed permanently. We could no longer ask our staff to risk the daily journey through Taliban checkpoints to attend work.

I was heartbroken and inconsolable that night. Think of me what you will. I called it and I must live with it. Nothing now will change that.

We needed a positive intervention. And hard work focuses the mind. We sourced the details of the potential chartered aircraft we would likely hire and found an air cargo specialist to draw up the potential air-pallet load plan.

Apparently the cargo of any aircraft needs to be balanced. We set about practising the load plan by drawing the outline of the air pallet on the flat area in front of the clinic. I then tasked the team with practising the loading of each air pallet for time. For example, crate number five that contained Ragnar and Cora needed to be next to crate number eight, because they were both 102cm-sized, so we could fit another three that size on the pallet. Clearly we had crates of other sizes too, especially the cat crates, which were tiny compared to the 102cm-sized ones. So each pallet contained a differing number of animals and crates. Once the team thought they nailed the load in good order, I would grin madly at them and say "Yak dafa degam" (One more time).

They actually became pretty good at an exercise they would sadly never carry out in real life.

17 August 2021

The screams and shouts were terrifying. The soldiers' commands, shouted in English, occasionally rode over the din.

"GET BACK!" ordered the Corporal of the Guard, rallied with his men in a defensive line, baton shields raised. "GET FUCKING BACK!"

These young soldiers had not served in Northern Ireland – that conflict had long since ended. They had no experience of riot control and had been thrust into this hastily arranged evacuation that lacked the clear oversight needed from the grown-ups back in the United Kingdom, bearing in mind the Foreign Secretary had remained on holiday.

In front of them, in the dark of the night sky, a line of SUV-type vehicles formed a barrier, one car with the passenger door wide open. Abandoned. An Afghan man stood on the roof of an empty vehicle, shouting incomprehensively toward the crowd. A lone black wheelie suitcase, its handle extended and upright stood discarded in the middle of the two opposing groups of people. Litter lay everywhere.

Suddenly the *BANG BANG BANG* of shots being fired into the air reverberated around the enclosed blast walls of the narrow road leading to the Abbey Gate entrance and the Baron Hotel. Coiled razor wire topped the concrete barricades forming either side of the road. Once caught in the throng of panicked Afghans heading towards the gate, you had little chance of turning around.

The surging wave of Afghans, desperate to get into the airport, paused briefly as the bullets flew in an arc high into the air, before surging again. The hastily tossed tear-gas grenade exploded, emitting an irritant cloud that affected the eyes of anyone within range. The painful stinging sensation rendered your eyes incapacitated should you keep them open, and rubbing them only made it worse. Inhaling the gas was a game-over moment as it affected the upper respiratory tract, resulting in severe coughing, choking, and sometimes nausea. You were completely debilitated.

A woman, draped in a long white headscarf and clutching two small rucksacks, wandered aimlessly in the confusion, unsure where to head. Towards the defensive line of British troops or backward into the crush of her fellow Afghans? A young man with a child held close to his chest ran forward and disappeared into the fog of choking tear gas.

And somewhere in that surging sea of people were my Kaisa and Najwa with her family. Najwa had to leave. She was thirty-four-weeks pregnant and vulnerable. If she went into labour in Kabul, then none of us were going anywhere. We had decided that their only option was to make an attempt for the airport at the height of the evacuation. We could not wait to see if Operation Ark would provide a means for them to be evacuated.

With all commercial flights cancelled, they had no choice but to attempt to flee on an evacuation flight provided by the military. But first they had to actually get into – as in inside the compound of – the airport. And that meant passing through one of the three gates into the airport being used for the evacuation. And these gates were choke points that would eventually prove to be fatal.

I wasn't there. But my very good friend Canadian Dave was. He was sending me live video feed from his vantage position on the roof of the Baron Hotel. He had been there for nearly a week helping to evacuate Canadian-registered citizens through the back of the Baron Hotel so they could slip more easily through the Abbey Gate, at times much to the annoyance of the British commander.

It had been my call for Kaisa, Najwa, and her family to try the Abbey Gate.

The Abbey Gate wasn't the first attempt. They had originally tried to gain entry to the airport via the East Gate, one of the two American-controlled gates. Afghans in their thousands were milling around the entrance to the gate, Taliban fighters wandering around the outer edges of the crowd. As Najwa was American, the East Gate still seemed the most reasonable, plus safest and easiest.

Through a series of contacts (someone who knew someone), I managed to blag the cell phone number of the current commander on the ground controlling the access to the East Gate. As Kaisa, along with Najwa and Mirwais shielding their three-year-old son, Ibrahim, fought forward through the crowd towards the gate, I was asking the marine sergeant to keep an eye out for the four of them. He had heard about me from his mum back home of all things. He sounded like a good guy.

They were almost at the gate and held their passports high above their heads. Kaisa truly believed they would get in. The gate was opening just briefly to allow a military-clad arm to snatch a US passport holder inside the welcome sanctuary of the gate's interior.

The crowd behind Najwa and Kaisa surged. I could hear Kaisa yelling through the speaker of my English phone as I screamed into my other phone at the commander on the gate to eyeball the tall blonde woman and drag her inside.

Suddenly he refused, saying it was now too dangerous

to open the gate for anyone at all. I could hear screams and shouted commands echoing through the speaker. Without warning I heard a volley of shots ring out. Stunned, I yelled back into the phone, "What have you just done?"

He never replied. The phone line was now dead.

Najwa's family and Kaisa were directly in front of the gate. The surge of desperate people flowing one way meant they were in danger of being crushed against the steel gate that was meant to protect those on the other side. As the gunshots overhead rang out, the tightly packed throng of humanity panicked as one and the sway threatened all four of them.

The tactics and processes used to control the crowd were amateurish at best and at their worst would later prove fatal.

When all four of them had extricated themselves back to a safe distance away from the gate, Kaisa called me again. I was vastly relieved that they were safe. But we still had the problem of the pregnant Najwa. It was then that I had suggested that they work their way around to the Abbey Gate, as Canadian Dave was there and maybe he could assist them in gaining entry.

I had no idea that directing them to the Abbey Gate would put them in so much danger until it was too late.

–

I was in the Nowzad office, an undrunk and now-cold cup of tea in front of me as I shouted down the phone to Canadian Dave, trying to make myself heard above the noise from his end of the conversation.

"Tell them to find the south wall and follow it along," Dave yelled back at me. "I'll meet them."

"Roger." I put him on mute, so that I wasn't distracted by

the gunfire and general yelling blasting out from the speaker.

I picked up my other phone and tried my best to sound calm. Kaisa was holding herself together, but I could hear the utter stress in her voice.

"Kaisa, head to south wall and follow it towards Abbey Gate. Dave is waiting for you," I yelled into the phone.

Kaisa knew Dave well too. We travelled across Kabul most Fridays to visit Dave and his wife, Junping, at their compound. Dave ran risk management and life support services for Western teams wishing to do business in Afghanistan. Along with secure accommodation they always had a good stock of Captain Morgan Spiced Rum. Christmases and birthdays had come and gone, and all had been celebrated there, even once whilst sitting through an earthquake.

"Pen," she yelled back, the desperation evident in her voice, "we can't. We are being crushed."

It was like the East Gate but worse. The crowd was heaving against the gate and walls, trying to get in. Mirwais was protecting little Ibrahim from being battered against the wall by the pushing and shoving crowd. Everyone had no choice but to look after themselves in that desperate situation. Except for Kaisa. She didn't look after herself. Najwa was in danger of her belly being crushed against the wall. Kaisa immediately used her body to shield Najwa as the crowd surged, pushing with her arms and legs back against the wave of human bodies to keep any pressure from Najwa. Kaisa protected Najwa throughout.

I felt completely helpless. There was nothing I could do.

"We are leaving here." The phone line went dead as she hung up abruptly. I slammed the phone down onto the plastic-coated surface of the desk.

I am not sure I have ever felt such despair as I did in that moment.

I would not hear back from Kaisa until she was out of the densely-packed Abbey Gate approach road some thirty minutes later. Hours later, she, Najwa, and Najwa's family arrived back at the Nowzad compound, weary, emotionally drained, and very shell-shocked at what they had just survived.

I let Dave know of their decision. He sounded so frustrated too. "Keep safe, mate," I said to finish the conservation.

"You too, buddy," he replied, still with a background of gunfire and shouted commands.

Dave stayed right until the end to facilitate the evacuation of as many families as he could. There are many a family now living in Canada who owe their new lives to Dave.

I never knew until many months after the evacuation of what happened that night in amongst that carnage. Kaisa only told me once, and then would never talk about it again. And neither will I.

Looking back, I should have done something more. Now and probably always, I struggle with what I didn't do.

She was not the same person when she finally returned. Writing this breaks my heart all over again. I should have been with her.

18 August 2021

Naively, we had assumed that the emergency debate on Afghanistan held in the House of Commons on that Wednesday would provide the permissions we desperately sought to land our chartered aircraft in Kabul, grant our staff the required paperwork to board, and allow them to travel to England. Our whole team crammed excitedly into our small living room on the upstairs floor of the house to watch. I had connected my laptop to the television screen.

Sara Britcliffe, Member of Parliament for Hyndburn, who just for full disclosure I have never met, raised our predicament during the debate directly with the Prime Minister. She was doing so on behalf of her own constituents who had pressed her to do so.

Najwa translated as Boris responded, "And we will do everything we can to help Mr Pen Farthing and others who face particular difficulty like himself."

The room erupted in cheers. The Operation Ark campaign that we had started with the emotionally charged interview with Phil Lassman had not just been to raise the large sum of money needed to charter an aircraft. We also needed our huge supporter base to email, ring, and write to their MPs in a bid to have our team added to the list of vulnerable Afghans considered for evacuation.

Our supporters had answered the call to action and then some! For a moment we thought it was in the bag when Boris said the magic words, "And we will do everything we can to help Mr Pen Farthing."

–

Meanwhile, a section of the Taliban had moved into the vacated fire station. It would not be long before we were paid a visit. We were sure of that. Rumours were rife of Taliban intelligence services hunting down former senior government employees. As a former Royal Marine who had fought the Taliban and whose charity worked with the local government, it was absolutely reasonable that I could be on a list.

Just the day before, Farid and I had braced ourselves when a knock sounded on the compound gate. Our security cameras displayed two trucks disembarking heavily armed fighters right outside our compound.

"Ok, here we go."

I sucked it in as I led Farid to the front gate, our female staff running upstairs to change into their long black figureless dresses and swap into thick dark headscarves.

As we stood behind the gate awaiting the shouted commands to open, the trucks' engines gunned to life as the Talib fighters remounted the vehicles. They sped off. Who knows why. But I assumed we had just witnessed a hunting party.

The relief was a tad overwhelming to be honest.

Despite the boost in optimism after hearing the PM's promise, the feeling that there was no way out was growing.

19 August 2021

I stood in the shadow of the gate as a nondescript car pulled up in front of the Nowzad compound, dust swirling behind it. Behind the dirty and cracked windscreen the bearded driver gave no acknowledgement that I was even there.

Mirwais, who was stood with me, leant forward and opened the passenger door to briefly chat with the driver.

"Our driver," he confirmed as he closed the door again.

I stepped back through the threshold of our pedestrian gate, cut into the wide vehicle doors that formed the entrance to the Nowzad clinic, and smiled at the figures standing there waiting patiently.

Both Kaisa and Najwa were dressed in long baggy tops that went down to their knees, black headscarves hiding their hair. Ibraham was clutching his mother's hand tightly. I quickly knelt and gave him one last cuddle. "See you in America, dude," I said quietly even though I knew he didn't really understand English. But if all went well, he soon would. Najwa would make sure of that.

I quickly stood up and hugged Najwa. "Be safe." I truly meant it, but my words seemed lame in the current circumstances.

"You too," she replied.

I turned to face Kaisa. We had already said our heartfelt goodbyes in the house, away from prying eyes. I hugged her again. She hugged me back, hard.

"I love you. See you in Norge land, min søthet." I tried to sound reassuring and confident as I stared into her sad blue eyes. Inwardly, I was anything but.

"You had better, my Pen," she replied in that angelic

accent of hers which got me every time I heard her. I loved that bloody accent. I smiled and nodded.

Without further hesitation, Kaisa stepped out from the Nowzad compound for the final time and slid into the waiting car next to Najwa.

Mirwais took up the free passenger seat with Ibrahim snuggly on his lap. The bearded driver pulled away. I stood and watched them drive to the junction with the fire station, now home to some random Taliban unit, before they turned left and disappeared as they headed to wherever it was that this "taxi" service was operated from.

I felt numb as I stared at the now-empty road. I looked down at the ground and briefly allowed myself to feel despair. I had no idea what was going to happen next and as I stood there, vulnerable out in the open, I took a moment to wonder if I would ever see Kaisa's beautiful smile again.

"Well, you definitely won't if you stand out here," I chided myself. I turned abruptly and headed back into the compound, closing and locking the pedestrian gate behind me.

Just how we managed to "order" that taxi will have to remain undisclosed. Let's just say we knew a guy who knew a guy and no, it wasn't Boris Johnson.

-

The young guy, with bushy blonde hair and sporting a well-grown beard stood confidently in front of the metalled entrance to the featureless compound. His tight T-shirt did nothing to cover his bulging bicep muscles. Maybe that was the point.

He was wearing well-worn chest armour with attached extra magazine pouches that held full topped-off spare mags for the compact M4 rifle draped across his chest. His sling set-up supported the weapon in the "ready to fire" position, his right hand gently gripping the pistol grip, right forefinger placed over the trigger guard to prevent any accidental discharge of the weapon. With no identifying unit patches, it screamed he was a special operative. His secondary weapon, a 9mm pistol strapped to his hip on the outside of his faded denim jeans, only enhanced the impression.

As Najwa and Kaisa's "taxi" arrived, he raised his weapon, the muzzle ready to discharge its deadly load directly into the front windshield of the car.

Najwa, Mirwais, and Kaisa all tensed. Having a loaded weapon pointed directly at you is never something you want to experience for yourself.

When the driver, who had still not uttered a word, slowed to a stop, the operator kept his weapon raised as he walked to the side of the vehicle. The driver lowered the side window carefully.

Relaxing just slightly as he quickly identified the occupants of the car, he leant forward as he lowered his weapon back to the ready position. "I hear y'all need a ride?" he said with a smirk and an American accent, not too harsh to be a New Yorker but not as soft as a local from South Carolina.

Based on the glowing portrayal I received many months later, I am going with the belief that the relief of seeing a friendly face, and the route he offered to freedom, biased their recollections of him. Apparently, his chiselled features were an understatement.

Of course they were, I'd thought to myself with just a hint of jealously.

Whilst the base was meant to be covert and hidden, here

he stood in full view as the Taliban swarmed across the country reasserting their authority. And he seemed to care not a hoot.

As he moved swiftly to the side, the gate behind him opened and he ushered the vehicle forward. After a swift look behind him to check there were no further vehicles headed along the isolated track towards this compound, he proceeded inside.

As their car drove in through the entrance way to what was an unassuming compound from the outside, the gate closed behind them with a metallic clap as the deadbolts were driven home.

"As we drove in through the entrance gate, we immediately realised just how huge this compound was," Najwa explained as she recounted the story to me, many months later when I flew to New York to visit her, Mirwais, Ibrahim, and my new "niece" Sahar.

"Either side of the road that divided the compound, in what were football-sized fields, sat row after row of Afghan soldiers. All cross-legged. Just sat there." Both Kaisa and Najwa still seemed somewhat shocked by the sight that had greeted them.

You must remember that just outside these walls the Taliban were searching high and low for former Afghan government employees and military commanders.

Yet they both estimated that nearly 2,000 were sitting patiently, seemingly calm and relaxed, cross-legged in neat rows. In the distance, a large military helicopter was being loaded with Afghan soldiers from the end of the rows nearest to it. As soon as it was loaded to capacity, it would power up and with its nose down, lift gracefully into the bright morning sky, quickly to be replaced by another helo.

Their vehicle never slowed, and they were driven farther along the road and deeper into the compound. Najwa marvelled that those who operated from here had performed an amazing job of remaining unknown even to the locals. Mirwais' family lived around the area that they now found themselves in and nobody had been aware of the existence of this extensive and secretive compound.

Their driver and the operator, who had by now squeezed into the car with them, directed them to a row of portacabins. Afghan faces peered out at them through the fabricated buildings' tiny windows.

"Phones, please," the operator directed. "You can have them back when you leave," he confirmed as his outstretched hand waited patiently.

Once he was happy with the haul of three phones, he opened the door for them all to enter. The eight-by-ten foot room was sparsely furnished with Afghan furniture – a simple single bed, a few hardback wooden chairs, and a desk. Kept clean and tidy, it would do as a respite from the slowly building heat of the day as they waited for the next phase of the operation to transport them into Kabul airfield. A small shower and toilet were in a false-walled corner of the unit.

Why the Taliban forces, who were swarming around Kabul, chose to ignore the operations of this compound, I can only speculate. Months after the evacuation, watching CNN Online, I viewed a reporter film a news piece from the ruins of a covert Central Intelligence Agency base that had been located north of Kabul airport. The video clip I watched matched the description of the compound that Najwa and Kaisa had given.

The ability to operate the compound at the height of the evacuation, outside of the safety perimeter of the Western forces protecting Kabul airport, had been tolerated because, I guess, a deal had been struck. How else could a poorly defended compound be allowed to operate a continuous helicopter taxi service into the evacuation hub of Kabul airport?

Najwa, feeling the toll of being thirty-four-weeks pregnant, shotgunned the bed with Ibrahim. They were all left to their own devices for several hours, drifting in and out of fitful sleep until they were awoken by explosions.

Startled and somewhat worried, they crammed to look out of the small portacabin windows to find the source of the bangs. Troublingly, they could see no resulting cloud mushrooming into the sky, but it could have come from anywhere within the vast compound.

A rapid knock at the door startled them. The instigator didn't wait to be invited in. It was the operator with the bushy blonde hair from earlier. "Sorry," he offered as he stepped over the threshold and into the portacabin. "We had to destroy some equipment, should have warned you." He smiled happily as he said it. "Anyway, folks. Your helo is here."

And with that, Ibrahim, Najwa, Mirwais, and Kaisa all experienced their first and probably only ride in a heavy-lift Chinook helicopter for the four whole minutes it took to fly low over the boundary fence of Kabul airport and swoop in to land at the military terminal in the northern half of Kabul airport.

They were inside the perimeter walls of the airport. They were safe.

Najwa and her family were immediately singled out as they descended the tail ramp of the helo and directed towards the American evacuees processing area. A quick hug to say goodbye was all they were afforded. As Kaisa was Norwegian, she was left to stroll awhile alone through the maze of abandoned buildings and storage containers, doors wide open to reveal discarded rubbish and empty boxes that made up the once vibrant and extremely busy northern military side of the airport.

Eventually she located the Norwegian medical tent, the Norwegian flag flying proudly from its flagpole.

She told me that she noticed immediately the queue for processing by the Norwegian embassy staff was somewhat short: just five other eligible passengers, which included an Afghan-Norwegian journalist she knew and two Norge embassy staff she'd met at the Norwegian National day celebrations back at the embassy in May. Overzealously they had all marched around the embassy carpark to the strains of the Norwegian anthem whilst waving national flags, much to the amusement of the Swedish embassy that shared the grounds. Now, they waited together for over four hours to board a flight that would take her far away from me and the approaching tidal wave of strict change that was being forced upon Afghanistan.

Her chariot to freedom had been parked on the runway the entire duration of the delay.

Let me repeat that: they waited for over four hours to board a plane that was parked on the runway throughout.

So much for the constant messaging we were receiving from the British government that any privately chartered aircraft I intended to land at the airport would jeopardise the precise timelines of the military evacuation operations.

"Hi, honey," I yelled into the phone as I sat sweltering in

the un-airconditioned Nowzad office. "Are you any closer to leaving?" It was already seven in the evening in Kabul, the helicopter having dropped her in to the airport over six hours ago.

Her voice sounded so far away. "Not yet, my Pen," she replied. "We are still waiting for the crew to find passengers to take up the available seating."

The aircraft carrying my wife to safety belonged to the Strategic Airlift Capability (SAC), a multinational initiative which guaranteed military airlift capability in a time of need. Norway was a member. And this was most definitely a time of need if there ever was one.

The SAC, established in 2008, operated three hugely capable C-17 Globemasters based out of Pápa Air Base in Hungary. The huge sky-grey coloured tail fin of the aircraft bore the insignia "Pápa 02" which denoted it was the second of the three SAC aircraft. With a payload capability of around 130 seated passengers or, if reconfigured, a sixty-nine-ton M1 Abrams main battle tank, it was a *beast* of an aircraft.

And that was the issue.

How many times did I read in the papers or hear on the news that the Nowzad Operation Ark initiative would distract and prevent desperate Afghans, who had earnt their right to safe passage because of their connections to the military, from being evacuated?

Yet here was an aircraft that could carry over 130 desperate passengers but had just five. The aircrew explained to the lucky five that they had painstakingly spent the preceding hours physically reaching out to each nation's admin area for passengers to fill those glaringly empty seats.

None were pushed forward.

None.

Let that sink in.

The transport aircraft was waiting patiently with its enormous cargo ramp extended as the crew made their final pre-flight checks. The contrasting red and dark blue of the Norwegian flag erected from the lower end of the cargo ramp happily flapped in the evening breeze.

The aircraft's loadmaster was eager to board his passengers and be airborne. They had wasted enough time on the ground.

Kaisa looked out west across the end of the runway to take her final glimpse at the setting Afghan sun as it rapidly vanished behind the jagged peaks of Paghman district in the distance. She told me many weeks later she felt beyond sorrow in that moment. Everything she had worked so diligently for over the last two years in Kabul with its young and extremely brave girls had disintegrated before her eyes. Young Afghan women with hopes and dreams that had flourished under Kaisa's watchful eye and gentle encouragement were now scattering to the winds in their own attempts to escape Kabul. Once feted as potential leaders within their own communities, they were on the run for their lives, and none of us had any real idea where they were or where they would end up.

I shared Kaisa's pain. They had been my friends too and some had treated me like their older brother. We had danced and laughed together.

The opening for her to leave was a one-time-only opportunity. Convincing her to leave had been hard for both of us but keeping Kaisa even for a minute more in Kabul would have been an act of utter selfishness on my part.

I loved her immeasurably. And that meant I had to let her go.

Taking Kaisa out of the picture ensured my ability to truly focus on the task in hand. I knew I operated better alone. And yet in reality I would not be on my own. I had over sixty lives depending on my decisions and my ability to keep it all together, and of course lots of dogs to keep me amused.

In my heart of hearts, I knew I would see her again. I had no doubt about that. Even if I had to walk across the bloody Kyber Pass into Pakistan to do so, I would see my wife again.

Taking one last look at a view she would never experience again, Kaisa walked up the ribbed cargo ramp of the Globemaster, her small daysack strapped over her right shoulder carrying just the basics she needed for the journey home.

The darkness of the early Kabul night was replaced by the ambient green glow of the operational military transport cabin as she entered. After a quick formal brief amidst the whine of the hydraulics lifting the huge cargo ramp into its closed position, Pápa 02 thundered down the runway and its four Pratt and Whitney engines powered it into the darkened night sky of Kabul.

Cocooned in its belly, five people, just *five* people, were carried that night to safety.

Kaisa had just texted me to say that the aircraft had started to taxi along the runway, so I quickly responded with "Safe flight. Love you, min søthet," and placed my phone on the desk. I bent down to scoop up a sleeping Ewok and carried the little ball of fluff gently out onto the balcony that had been the focal point of our evenings drinking wine or playing games during the countless hot summer nights we had spent in Kabul.

I looked skyward and stared at the crystal-clear night sky whilst rubbing Ewok's belly. His little eyes stared up into the night whilst he made these endearing cooing noises. Now and again in the background, the still of the night would be punctured by a dog barking for no good reason I could identify before quietness once more reigned supreme.

Kabul is most definitely an ideal place if you want to stargaze. With limited street lighting there's no light pollution to diminish the viewing experience. A million tiny pinpoints of light stared back down at me as I took time to marvel the spectacle above.

In the distance, I could hear an intensifying low roar as the aircraft carrying my world powered up through its ascent. And then the flashing tail-light and the darkened shadow arced high above my head as the C-17 roared through its ascent and disappeared amongst the stars. She truly could have been on a starship, heading into outer space. We were now worlds apart.

I felt empty. Kaisa was gone.

I stayed staring longingly into the night sky for a while. Ewok had easily fallen asleep in my arm. The little bugger could sleep.

I could have gone with her.

But of course, I did not. My staff and their families needed me. They had no out except for me. And little Ewok, what about him and daft boy Ragnar and sweet Cora and all the others? Should I just abandon them all to a fate unknown?

I couldn't have lived with myself. I had to stay and see this thing through.

My emotions raged. I was in complete turmoil. Part of me was jubilant and relieved that my beautiful wife was no longer on the ground in harm's way in Kabul, yet the anger and bitterness I felt towards the evacuation's unfolding chaos was unmatched. I wanted to scream out loud.

None of this had to happen: chaos at the gates, the lack of permissions, planes leaving effectively empty. The frustration and anger I felt was overwhelming. I carried Ewok back to my office and tapped the box of red wine strategically placed on the edge of my desk for another glass of its soothing liquid.

After calming myself and considering my options, I picked up my phone and dialled the number I had for the BBC to voice my displeasure at the continued shitshow that was unfolding daily.

The photos of Kaisa's empty aircraft gained international attention after I had voiced my displeasure via my social media channels.

It wasn't just the SAC's C-17 Globemaster which travelled shockingly empty.

On the 24th of August, the Independent published an article headlined *Afghanistan: Anger as car airlifted out of Kabul amid evacuation operation – images surface online amid fears some will be left behind in Kabul.*

Written by Matt Mathers, a photo was inserted directly under the headline. Clearly taken from inside a military transport aircraft, it depicted some brand of silver SUV without registration plates, securely strapped down to the rear cargo ramp. Soldiers were seen leaning against the side of the vehicle and they were clearly identifiable as British due to the style of the military combat fatigues they were wearing. I think my prior experience can, without much doubt, lend me as a credible witness to that.

Either side of the vehicle in the jump seats situated along

adjacent sides of the aircraft were Afghan evacuees. They stared at the floor or just looked directly ahead, eyes vacant, shellshocked. Everything they had ever known was being left behind and that in most cases included extended family members and friends.

Devoid of any baggage, they were only able to escape with what they were wearing. And towards the front of the aircraft were many more cross-legged Afghans crammed in neat rows across the full width of the military cargo aircraft, holding on tightly to cargo straps tensioned across each rank as a makeshift seatbelt. Allowing people to sit on deck had never been an original design point and probably had given the loadmaster a few grey hairs to safely arrange his charges for the flight.

At least the vehicle was securely held in place.

This aircraft had been used to "rescue" a vehicle which, by my rough calculations from studying the photograph, took up space that could have been filled by at least sixty evacuees.

Compared to that, I had no stomach for further accusations of wasting space on any aircraft to evacuate our animals. We weren't even using a military aircraft. We had secured funding for our own private chartered flight. It could easily carry 230 passengers, maybe more if evacuees sat in the aisles, and of course, our animals would be loaded into the cargo hold.

The Nowzad tally of potential evacuees numbered sixty-seven. We had space for an extra 169 desperate people fleeing the fate that was now about to befall Afghanistan.

"Unreal!" I screamed as I read the article. Ewok, deep in slumber in the afternoon heat, had woken with a jolt, his head turned towards me, to confirm the source of the disturbance.

To say I was raging was an understatement. The delay in granting us permission to move our staff to the airport just did not make sense.

We had demonstrated the risk our staff faced: they had worked closely with coalition forces. I hated having to justify what I felt was our team's right to be evacuated over other needy Afghans determined to flee a future under the Taliban. But during those initial days of the evacuation, the British government airlifted thousands who had just broken through the gates and fences back on the 15th and 16th of August when the airport had been overrun. Neither interpreters nor aides to the former military presence in Afghanistan, they were just desperate people, mostly young men, who took the initiative or followed the herd and made the desperate scramble for the airport before the cordons were put in place. I can't say I blame them. But equally, did nobody appreciate we had sixty-eight Afghan people with just as much right if not more to board a flight?

I had been on the go for ten days, my accumulated daily sleep stretching to three to four hours at most. Regular food stops were few and far between. Writing this, I cannot remember making a single meal. I have no idea what I ate during the evacuation, probably protein bars and cheese sandwiches.

Basically, I was fucking tired.

And that tiredness and frustration meant I would often tweet first and then once the comments or, more importantly, national news outlets reached out, would stop and think about it. By then it was always too late to edit or even delete a post.

Such was the anger and stress of the situation.

In an ideal world I would have had a highly trained marketing staff who carefully crafted posts and tweets, each of which would have been infinitely shareable. Instead Nowzad had me as its social media marketeer. Me in all my rage and exhaustion, full of anxiety for the staff and animals, frustrated and at a loss. Here's a tip: when you're in that headspace, don't use social media unless you're prepared for the blow-back.

A quote from the MoD spokesperson stated, "We are aware of reports around vehicles being loaded onto flights leaving Afghanistan. Cleared passengers are always loaded as an absolute priority and any spare capacity is used for operational freight. No flight has left Kabul empty."

If this statement were true then the question is, why had the British government cleared so few passengers that there was room for a fucking car?

Many, including Ricky Gervais, shared their displeasure at the evacuation of a car. But Ben Wallace, the Defence Minister in charge of Operation Pitting and the evacuation, when asked for his response to the car being airlifted out, continued with the party line to promote the evacuation numbers: "Britain has so far evacuated more than eight thousand people from Afghanistan in the past ten days, including more than two thousand in the previous twenty-four hours." (As reported by Matt Mathers in his article).

The government's party line was echoed by swathes of the press.

LBC's James O'Brien refers to our system of governing as an ecosystem. It governs us through "deceit, division and distraction," including a lapse of scrutiny when it would be appropriate and necessary.

Constant opinion pieces stated how our charity would be the reason desperate Afghans and their families were left on the tarmac of Kabul airport. Some people even got it into their heads that I was friends with Carrie Johnson, the PM's wife, which was beyond absurd. On the other hand, I was critical of the government's evacuation. Whether someone was pro- or anti-government, there was a "reason" to dislike me.

Having said that, I never envisioned the abuse I would receive. Personal smears, abusive emails and phone calls, threats of violence. "Pen Farthing should be publicly horse-whipped" was one example from a prominent social media commentator. Actual death threats and untold promises of retribution in the next life.

I never reported to the police the two guys who sent me death threats and of course I clearly should have. But instead, I asked them where they wanted to meet. The always-cowardly keyboard warriors never responded.

20 August 2021

"You need how much?" was the astonished response from our chairman after my short brief. I stole a sideways glance towards my black thirty-ounce Yeti mug. Dinked and dented, it had literally been everywhere with me. But now it was just a useless metallic container.

100% due to the fact it was bloody empty.

I'd drained the last of its contents several minutes ago and stupidly left the wine box to top up my tumbler downstairs in our bedroom. I had severely screwed up on my prior preparation. Marines the world over would be mouthing, "Take an 'F' for fail, Farthing." Prior preparation does prevent poor performance. Something the British government should also have known.

It was early in the morning of the 20th. Very early. 2am my time. 10.30pm in the United Kingdom on the 19th. And, for our chairman in Texas, something like 4pm.

I looked at the two rows of non-emotional faces staring at me on the Zoom screen. "$80,000 dollars please." I smiled sarcastically as I reconfirmed my earlier request.

"How the hell are we going to get $80,000 in cash to you," was the perplexed query from another voice on the screen.

During those two weeks of August 2021, the evacuation committee and I Zoomed at least three to four times daily. I also took part in countless television and radio interviews with more media channels than I care to remember. To my utter amazement we never suffered a communication blackout once, although reports that the Taliban were going to cut the internet connection to Afghanistan were rife.

Now would have been a good opportunity to experience

one though. It would have been my excuse to trot downstairs and refill my mug.

"Team, I have no idea, can somebody please research it? Najwa mentioned Hawala payments might work?" Not that I had any idea what a Hawala payment was at that point.

With the complete collapse of the banking system due to Biden's imposed restrictions, there was no method for transferring funds into Afghanistan via any recognised and accepted financial system. Banks across Afghanistan had closed their doors on the 14th when the run on the banks began, as anyone with a bank account scrambled to withdraw their money. Mujtaba and Mirwais had spent nearly six hours in line to be told they could only withdrawal $100 from their own accounts. Our charity had nearly $50,000 now frozen in our charity account in the city.

$80,000 is clearly a lot of money. But we desperately needed it. We had no way to transport the ninety-four dogs and sixty-seven cats into the airport without it. Our rudimentary maths had worked out that we needed at least two decent flatbed lorries for the animals' transportation needs. We could hire them, but the lorries would most likely be driven by their owner-drivers, who would in no way be connected to Nowzad. This meant they would not appear on any official list to enter the airport. And that in turn meant that the lorries would not get through the checkpoints and the animals would not get to the plane we had chartered.

I was ignoring the fact that none of us currently had permission to enter the airport ourselves. I tried my hardest not to dwell on that.

Boris Johnson had publicly promised we would receive the help we needed, but two days later we hadn't received so much as an email saying we'd be sent official permissions. I was not asking for any form of preferential treatment – but the Prime Minister had said he would support me publicly so I was kind of believing it would indeed happen.

Nagging doubt was creeping in.

–

Back to the lorry owners. The question remained: why would anyone who owed their livelihood to said lorries consider handing over the keys so we could jump in and drive them ourselves? Obviously, once we arrived at the flight line, our only priority would be loading the chartered aircraft, ensuring our staff were safely strapped in, and taking that evacuation flight out of Afghanistan. It would not be returning the trucks to the owners waiting patiently outside the airport perimeter.

Any lorry owner with a brain cell knew that.

No, our only choice would be to buy two trucks suitable for what we hoped would be a one-way trip. And to do that, I needed cold hard cash. Swiping a credit card and forgetting about it until the statement came in was not a thing in Afghanistan, this was a cash-only economy.

The staff had not been paid for July and whether Operation Ark worked or not, we also needed to pay them for August. In Afghanistan, as with most neighbouring countries, it was a financial system that lived day by day. Pension and savings schemes were not a viable option as nobody trusted anyone else with their hard-earnt money. And, most likely, everyone on our team would have been the sole breadwinner for their entire extended family. With the Afghan economy trending in a downward spiral combined with unemployment numbers that were through the roof, you took what you earnt on the day and hoped it made do until next pay day.

And then there was the Nowzad donkey sanctuary. It needed funding to continue the care of its residents for who knew how long? It was a place of solitude and calm, located on the southern outskirts of Kabul, far removed from the hustle and bustle of Afghanistan's capital. I loved visiting it. It was home to nine donkeys, including Khushi. Born seven years ago to her mum Rosie in a stable housed within the dog shelter we had built at the time, Khushi had initially grown up believing she was a dog. Playtime would see her chasing some of the canine residents around in circles, her being no bigger than them. Super-friendly Khushi (meaning "happiness") was such a special soul. She was the only donkey in Afghanistan that had never worked a day in her life. Born free from that weighted chain around her neck.

And we had David, a fully grown bull who I'd rescued from a Koochi nomad camp. David had been just a young calf, tied to a stake amongst the cluttered discarded waste in the corner of the camp, destined for a slow death from the infection that was ravaging his body when I had discovered him. He had been on the receiving end of a dog bite on the lower part of his front leg, which had not been treated. Bundling the nervous and still very strong animal into the back of our Nowzad van once we had removed the seating was a feat and a half. But the stress of that journey was now long forgotten by all as David, now a proper bull size, happily munched carrots from his carer's hands.

And along with two former working horses who now call the sanctuary home, we have JaJa the goat. Rescued from the same Koochi camp as David, JaJa lives out his days watching the world go by from the safety of his sheltered accommodation in the sanctuary.

When I rescued them, I promised both they would never be destined for a cooking pot. But with the arrival of the Taliban I could not guarantee that.

Four more of our staff had come forward to stay behind. They wanted to ride out the chaos and confusion as the Taliban retook Afghanistan. Their families were here. I promised I would do what I could to continue to pay them if they continued to look after the donkey sanctuary until I and the charity could return to Afghanistan. But when that would be I had no idea.

We had known outright that it would be impossible to evacuate our donkeys. This was the only option I had. Trusting the staff who had chosen to remain behind was all I could do. At any time, Taliban fighters could demand to be let into the sanctuary and if feeling hungry, well, it would be game over.

The Zoom meeting with the board finally ended. I had failed to secure the cash or more wine, which was probably for the best anyway. Stumbling onto my bed in sheer exhaustion, I was asleep before my head hit the pillow.

21 August 2021

The poshest-sounding army officer I had ever heard sent me a voice note at 0655hrs (Kabul Local) on the 21st of August 2021.

This is an exact transcript of the messages. His were voice notes and mine were simple texts in reply.

> Hi Pen, this is the half colonel in charge of the Baron Hotel force protection and security for the ARAP (Afghan Relocation and Assistance Policy) process. It has come to my attention that you are trying to facilitate yourself and a bunch of individuals through the rear gate, which is going to significantly impinge on our ability to continue the ARAP process going.
>
> I need to find out a few things from you. First and foremost, I need to understand whether the other individuals are entitled persons, by which I mean, they applied for ARAP and have been confirmed with an email which is asking them to turn up for biometric enrolment, or are they British visa holders or British passport holders. If they are not, then they are not entitled and they are not coming into the Baron Hotel.

(Aside: An ARAP was for people who had assisted the British government in a meaningful way or who had been exposed to Western forces in such as a way as to endanger them. It meant that they were entitled to evacuation.)

I listened intently to the voice note once more. How come he didn't know that the Nowzad staff were not British visa or passport holders? Was communication that bad between London and the ground? After all he must have been given my number by somebody back home in Westminster.

But for once I measured my response.

> Hi Boss, this will be coming directly from the PM. Linking you up now with the relevant people.

What else could I say? I was still waiting to receive the official documents that had been promised days ago.

His response:

> To be clear I am taking my orders from the Joint Task Force commander, and I am not taking my orders from anyone else outside of my military chain. I need you to let me know so that I can inform my chain of command the details of your people that you are trying to bring in.

Yet again I played it cool, despite my frustration bubbling. I had the sinking feeling that Boris Johnson had only made his promise in the House of Commons in order to placate Sara Britcliffe. This all but confirmed it.

Nonetheless, I tried.

> Boss, it will come down from above. Everyone is entitled. Ex-Royal by the way. Twenty-two years. Not going to do anything stupid to risk your guys' safety.

I had no intention of putting any British soldiers in harm's way or even wasting their time. I had always said I would get my myself and my team to the airport. The British government had already put them in harm's way with its disorganisation.

As soon as I had sent my above reply another voice note landed in the conversation.

> As I am sure you are aware the front gate is a melee where just as entitled individuals are being killed in a crush and this is what I am trying to deal with. I need you to be patient and if you can provide the proof through my chain of command you are bringing entitled persons in, then at the appropriate tactical time I can get my team to help facilitate.

He was beginning to really wind me up. He called the chaos at the front gate a "melee." I already knew about the fucking melee. Najwa and Kaisa had nearly been crushed to death in it. Most frustrating of all, he was asking for proof which I'd been promised but I still didn't have.

Eight days after I had first asked publicly for permission to evacuate the Nowzad staff, and three days since Boris Johnson had said we would receive the help we needed, nobody had yet made an official decision on paper.

Three days. What was taking so long to approve a permission for our vets and their families? We had the Taliban literally knocking on our door.

I told him the truth, hoping he had a conscience and would sympathise and genuinely help out – somehow.

> Roger that. I am not moving anywhere until I know somebody is unlocking the door. And yes, I know about the front – my wife was crushed there 4 days ago.

He read the message at 0706hrs (Kabul Local) and then I never heard again from the extremely posh-sounding half colonel during the evacuation.

While the day started poorly, it picked up dramatically. Kaisa finally touched down in Oslo to a whirlwind of local and national news cameras lined up outside the airport to capture her reunion with her relieved mum. Even the BBC ran a short segment covering it, such was the interest. I watched the shaky news clip, recorded on Rune's phone from the family television. In the background a Norwegian presenter described the scene.

I welled up watching her mum, who had been deaf since birth and sadly losing her sight, hug her daughter as they signed their relief to see each other again.

My Kaisa was home. A huge weight had been lifted from my shoulders. That the woman I loved was now safe and with her parents meant that I could breathe a little more easily. Now more than ever, I needed to concentrate on the rather large problem that demanded to be addressed: just how the hell were we going to get 171 dogs and cats, and 67 staff into the airport?

I had tasked Farid with conducting daily recces of the gates – taking photos and looking at the number of people surrounding the gates at various times of the day. We wanted as clear a picture as possible so, when the time came, we were fully prepared and stood the best chance of gaining entry. All the information pointed to just how difficult it would be to get into Kabul airport with that many people.

21 – 23 August 2021

Najwa's Story

Just because Najwa and her family had finally made it into Kabul airport sadly did not mean they had a straightforward journey to America... far from it.

Having left Afghanistan on a military flight, they landed in Qatar with hundreds of other Afghan refugees fleeing their homeland. Then they boarded another flight to Ramstein Air Base, southwest Germany. Once it landed, they were quickly herded down the cargo ramp of the military aircraft. The aircraft's loadmaster was frantically attempting to offload the human cargo as quickly as he could. Refuelling had already begun. Being on the clock meant it was his responsibility to get the aircraft back in the air and heading back to Qatar.

The United States' fragile deal with the Taliban required the implementation of a very tight schedule to evacuate all who needed to be by the 31st of August. Flying back-to-back sorties was the only way to even attempt an evacuation of this scale. There was no precedent to work from. This was all new territory.

Mirwais had never been to Europe before, and I am not sure this visit counted towards his holiday bucket list as, even though he was physically in Germany, he was on American territory. The laws surrounding who owns a foreign country's military base, whether it's the occupying military force operating from the base or the actual host country, are rather complex. For the sake of argument, let's say Mirwais was on German soil exclusively within the perimeter fence of an American airbase. Either way, I doubt he will ever want to visit again after the experience he was about to have courtesy of the unprepared service men and women serving at Ramstein.

Ramstein is the home of the 86th Airlift Wing of the United States Airforce and is a sprawling complex, noted for being the largest US military community outside of the continental United States. The air wing itself is enormous and spans four European countries: Germany, Portugal, Spain, and Belgium. That's a fact I find slightly overwhelming to comprehend. It really is bloody huge! According to the 86th Airlift Wing's website, Ramstein Air Base serves as the "Global Gateway" to Europe and beyond, operating key power projection platforms critical to global operations.

Reading that struck a deep nerve about the lack of investment any British government had given our armed forces over the last two decades. It made me envious of the United States' commitment to its armed forces. The United Kingdom is not even remotely the global power that we proudly once were. As a military we cannot even begin to compete with a tiny fraction of the heavy-lift capabilities that the United States has, let alone match any of its combat capabilities.

Over the preceding years, British governments from all parties have relentlessly forgone defence spending to the point that for seven years, Britain, once the leading global seafaring nation, essentially had no aircraft carrier. An island nation, which once ruled the seas, had been for a time a laughing stock amongst navies the world over.

Thankfully we now have two aircraft carriers commissioned, the *Queen Elizabeth II* and the *Prince of Wales*. However the government of the day bizarrely sold off our Harrier jump jet fleet, and financial constraints meant that we could not afford the F-35 Lightning aircraft needed to form either ship's air wing as the carriers were commissioned. So for many years we were sailing around with an aircraft carrier with no aircraft and even today as I write this, HMS *Queen Elizabeth* has deployed to the Middle East with just eight aircraft onboard when she should have a ship's compliment of thirty-three. Looking at Ukraine, I get a shiver of dread.

While America had the logistical might that we lacked, it suffered from a lack of joined-up thinking. Trump/Biden/whoever you want to blame for the call to withdraw from Afghanistan, never put in place any coherent plan to see it through.

It's as if each cog of the evacuation wheel had no idea what was coming next and when.

Najwa and Mirwais were about to experience that for themselves. They found themselves wrongly labelled as refugees as they arrived at the Joint Military Processing Centre (JMPC) in Ramstein. As they stepped foot on American/German soil they were directed onto a bus which transported them to the processing centre, a long room that contained nearly ninety chairs, all lined up in a single row.

The processing room was bland and unpleasant. An American serviceman dressed in camouflage clothing, whose purpose of being worn was defeated by the very orange high-visibility vest he was forced to wear over the top of the fatigues, found time after several hours to process Najwa and Mirwais.

"Men to that bus through the door." He pointed Mirwais to follow the last Afghan man who had walked out the door of the processing room to board a waiting bus that would take them to the hastily erected tented accommodation for men.

"We are married. I am an American," Najwa said and

rapidly retrieved her passport from her rucksack's outer pocket.

"Sorry, Ma'am," the soldier politely replied whilst also probably very relieved that Najwa spoke English. "Orders are that all men are accommodated in one area and all women and children are in a hangar."

"But we are married and not refugees!" Najwa exclaimed.

"Nothing I can do about that," the soldier replied as he once more gestured for Mirwais to follow his order and leave the room.

The processing hall was not fit for purpose and the staff manning it were poorly prepared for the influx of desperate people now arriving, forced to abandon everything in a spilt-second decision. Najwa, clutching Ibrahim closely to her side, explained once more that she, Mirwais, and Ibrahim were United States passport holders and not refugees that needed processing. Mirwais even had a US immigration visa stamp that stated he was pending his immigration hearing for residency.

The military orderly managing the ill-prepared processing facility was having none of it. Najwa and Ibrahim were duly processed, issued with blue-coded wrist bands, and directed to the women and children's area that had been arranged inside an enormous aircraft hangar.

What Najwa and Mirwais were not aware of was that Ramstein had been a last-minute part of the evacuation plan. The airbase command had been just given hours to build a refugee processing centre that was already now home to 10,000 Afghans who had fled the arrival of the Taliban in Kabul.

And each day a never-ending stream of C-17 aircraft would descend, delivering hundreds more refugees to the mix of Afghans already waiting for the promise of a new life in America. Ramstein Air Base was not ready to take on the demands of an evacuation of this scale. To be clear, the problem did not lie with the soldiers. Senior US administration officials had known this evacuation was coming since early 2020. They knew before any of us did what day they were going to pull the trigger.

Row upon row of military cot beds were lined up parade-fashion and most were already taken by exhausted Afghan women attempting to entertain their children and make some sense out of the tiny living areas immediately surrounding their cot. There was no more than two feet between each bed.

And at the height of the Covid pandemic ravaging the world, Najwa and her family had just been jettisoned into a Covid breeding-ground from hell. Most Afghans were not vaccinated against the disease as supplying countries like Afghanistan was not one of the world's priorities during 2020 and 2021. I had ensured our staff were vaccinated. I needed them at work is the honest reason – we had animals to care for. And thankfully for Najwa that gave her some protection whilst in such proximity to so many unvaccinated women.

Mirwais on the other hand, wearing his newly acquired wristband, was directed to a heavy canvas military tent aligned along an edge of a runway. The sign pinned hastily to the outside revealed that the tent was designated number C-17. Upon entering Mirwais could see that the tent could just about accommodate ten cot beds with less personal space than what the women enjoyed.

Food was, as you would expect, unappetizing and the lines endlessly long. As soon as lunch was over, the queue had already formed for the evening meal.

The portaloos, placed to cater to the needs of the constantly arriving evacuees, were completely inadequate.

Najwa counted ten standing portaloos – or as she called them, "Porta-Johns", which somewhat made me smile – for her section of the women's area which numbered some 500 people.

"We are having to wait two hours to use the toilet." I could hear the desperation in Najwa's voice. "I have not seen Mirwais since yesterday."

Just to back up her story, my phone pinged in my ear alerting me to a WhatsApp message being downloaded.

I placed Najwa on speaker phone and thumbed to the new message. Sure enough there was a photo taken inside one of the porta-johns, human excrement and used toilet paper covered the floor and the blue-coloured plastic outer of the toilet bowl.

Yet-to-be-utilised toilet rolls and a few bottled waters were currently being stored in the urinal element. Bizarrely, the manufacturers of the modular toilet had seen fit to imprint a smiley face into the underside of the toilet lid, also moulded in blue-coloured plastic.

I would bet a million dollars that nobody was smiling whilst carrying out whatever it was they needed to in the cramped confines of that poop hell.

I winced as I surveyed the scene, probably for longer than I should have. The human shit on the floor was disgusting.

"That is just fucking evil," I said to myself. As a former Royal Marine I had lived through many a toilet misadventure: crapping into a bag whilst lying in a hide during a mission to identify enemy positions, or every Friday burning the accumulated crap deposited by fifty Royal Marines living off a diet of ration packs during our tour of duty in Now Zad, which is where my path to a life of animal rescue had begun. And once in a previous life, I volunteered to unblock, by hand, a drop toilet in Morocco for a group of teenage girls I was guiding through the Atlas Mountains for their summer holidays. That was rank. If you ever meet me, think about that as we shake hands.

But this shitshow at the Ramstein base was just bad planning and a lack of compassion by those in command. The toilets could have been rotated out for cleaning. The United States military were more than capable of achieving that. This was the largest airbase in Europe. They had the resources.

"They have not cleaned them for two days now."

The next photo that arrived depicted two US servicemen in their fatigues, again their original purpose removed by the oversized orange high-visibility jackets they wore. Mingling around them were Afghan men, all wearing sandals, but some wrapped in black and white spotted blankets that were not military issue.

"We have just had the second fistfight this morning and it is only 9.30 still." She sounded worried, and I could understand the reasoning for that. "People are getting frustrated. Second fight was over food. First one I don't know why."

I was sat at my desk in Kabul, the sun throwing high shadows on the wall behind me as it rapidly said goodbye to another day of treading water, no closer to gaining the permissions we needed to leave Kabul far behind us.

It didn't make sense. With an American passport she shouldn't have been detained there in the first place. And I had no clue what we could do to secure Najwa and her family's release from Ramstein. I also knew taking on another sort of rescue whilst in the middle of the fight of our lives to evacuate our sixty-seven staff and all the dogs and cats was madness.

Again, it's not like I had a genuine choice in the matter. Not really. I was responsible for her and her family's safety.

"Ok, we will get you out. Hang in there."

At thirty-four-weeks pregnant and with the stress of the situation, there was a high chance Najwa could go into labour any day. My phone was buzzing with kind-hearted folks with suggestions of congressmen and senators that I should be reaching out to. Except they were not taking calls even if their aides had promised me they would get back to me.

They never did.

I never stopped ringing and emailing for the rest of the day, whilst our evacuation team was still applying the pressure back home in England for our main mission. Having made no forward progress, I collapsed into an immediate, deep, but always too short, sleep, awaking just a few hours later to frantic and desperate texts from Najwa.

"Ibrahim is sick."

We needed help from the inside and that was literally what we received by way of a miracle called Meg.

I had no idea truly how to get support for Najwa, so I did the only thing that I could do and reverted to type. I put out an angry post on social media.

Meg had been a major in the United States military with service around the world and years of practical hands-on planning before becoming a government advisor to the Kosovo government. But now retired and living near Ramstein, she was extremely angry and disgusted, just as many of her former colleagues were, at the abruptness of the withdrawal from Afghanistan. As with me and the thousands of other veterans who had served in Afghanistan, we questioned the sacrifice made just to hand the country back to the very people we had wrestled it free from.

Meg immediately volunteered to support the evacuation effort and arrived at Ramstein in the early evening. She was tasked with working the "in-between space" between the Afghans' arrival and their entering the tented accommodation in the containment area, handing out refreshments and answering questions if she was able to. The most common being, "When do we go to America?" for which she could only answer, "Soon" with a "Hopefully" caveated to the end.

She became deeply depressed by the sadness of it all. Unable to sleep that night, Meg began scrolling through Facebook when she came across my cry for help. Meg reached out to our Nowzad volunteer, Ann, who at two in the morning was doing an astonishing job of juggling the craziness of our Facebook messages inbox, which was overflowing with concern and ideas of how to help.

After a three-way conversation between Ann, Najwa, and Meg, a meet was arranged for the following day for ten o'clock outside of the tent numbered twenty-three, in the containment area for the refugees' accommodation.

Clearly though, the first hurdle for Meg was that she was no longer active military and, as a result, could not legally enter the refugee tented area of the airbase. For most of us that would have been game over, but Meg was determined to have Najwa safely on her way to America. Although retired, having served in numerous challenging situations, she still acted with an aura of authority as a former officer.

Ethan Hunt from the "Mission Impossible" films would have been proud of Meg's exploit at the gates to the tented accommodation. Holding her military ID so that her finger covered the portion denoting she was retired, and taking advantage of the disorganised chaos of those coming and going in a frantic attempt to bring a semblance of order, Meg rocked up, dominating the situation. With the authority of somebody who had every right to be there, the low-ranking gate sentry was not prepared to take on a determined major, either active or retired. She was in. And amongst the background of thousands of disorientated evacuees, Meg found Najwa.

She'd already realised that the US government had created a disaster with no contingency planning. Watching the desperation inside the tented accommodation and the helplessness on the faces of both the evacuees and the military tasked with making sense of it, Meg could see that nobody knew what was happening or what to do about it.

Meg knew she had to work the people to get Najwa and her family out of the misery of the transit camp.

During Meg's years of service in the Balkans, she had been touched by the plight of the stray dogs she saw there, so much so that she stayed on after her tour finished to rescue abandoned animals from the war-torn streets. She used that compassion to connect to the people who could be the difference in ensuring Najwa, an American citizen thirty-four-weeks pregnant, was transferred out of what was a refugee hellhole.

There wasn't a lot I could do but read the text messages between Ann, Kaisa, Najwa, and Meg as the great escape played out. To say I was in awe of Meg is something of an understatement. Team Meg was all positive can-do stuff.

Taking Najwa out of Ramstein Air Base to a nearby civilian airport like Frankfurt and booking them onto a commercial flight to America sounded like the smart solution. But it was immediately quashed. To leave Germany on an international flight, Najwa, Mirwais, and Ibrahim would have to be processed through the European passport control system, the same as you or me arriving in Germany from England. They needed an entry stamp so they could be given an exit stamp. Meg quickly realised they did not have one due to the fact they had arrived at an American airbase as *refugees*. The second they stepped outside of the airbase they would now be deemed to be illegal immigrants and arrested.

The US bureaucrats, attempting to figure out the next step in the chaos they had created, were oblivious to the fact that they had an American citizen, heavily pregnant and separated from her husband. They were running a clusterfuck of a show.

Meg knew it was down to her to get Najwa and her family the hell out of there.

Meg kept us updated via her texts to the newly formed Facebook Messenger group chat.

"I went to the admin tent. There I got in a disagreement with a representative from the US state department, as it was abundantly obvious that processes to push forward the evacuees had not been established. But we quickly moved passed the disagreement once we both realised we had a mutual friend that rescued dogs in Albania. I explained to her the situation Najwa was in and she went into action."

Meg convinced Najwa to head to medical and with Kaisa's help, they both convinced Najwa to hide her tough personality and play the needy game, ensuring the medical team recognised Ibrahim's and her own medical condition as a way of quietly securing their exit from the secure containment area.

State department reps pushed Najwa's priority level to the highest possible and within two hours the family had been manifested onto the very next flight leaving for Dulles later that day. But Najwa needed a fit-to-fly certificate due to her advanced pregnancy and so back to the medical tent they were sent. A lot of persuading was needed for the doctor to sign off on the fact that Najwa was fit to fly. The alternative, if no certificate had been issued, was that Najwa would have been consigned to the next five weeks in that camp.

Even Najwa was kept in the dark by Meg to ensure she wouldn't reveal their imminent departure to those around them. Any sudden excitement could have given the game away.

Air force police escorted Meg to find Najwa, where they made a show of ordering Najwa to gather her belongings whilst telling her she, along with Mirwais and Ibrahim, were being moved to a family tent. Meg could see the confusion etched on Najwa's face. She had no idea what was about to happen.

With thousands of frustrated Afghans demanding to be placed on a flight to America, they had to ensure Najwa, Mirwais, and Ibrahim were transported to the departure gate from the camp without fanfare. A stampede by several hundred people was not going to end well.

Hugging her, Meg whispered to Najwa, "Just play along, show no excitement, but we are taking you out of here now."

Reversing a passenger van up against the rear fence that had just been opened, base personnel loaded Najwa and her family into the van. There was to be no family tent for them. They were being driven directly to the departure gate.

At 2200 hrs (UK Local) on Monday the 23rd of August 2021, Najwa, Mirwais, and Ibrahim boarded a Delta flight for the United States of America.

Meg was officially a legend, and she stayed on working with others who needed help within the chaos of the constantly swelling camp as more evacuees arrived daily. In the time it took to facilitate the release of Najwa, thirty-two babies were born to evacuated Afghan families in the makeshift medical facilities of Ramstein's military processing centre.

Baby Sahar was born just five weeks later on the 30th of September in the Land of Opportunity. And if she follows even slightly in her mother's footsteps then the world will be just a little better for it.

22 August 2021

The details were sparse but apparently the Taliban, who had been operating their own perimeter outside the British security cordon, had fired their weapons to drive back the overwhelming crowds heading in the direction of the Abbey Gate corridor. The opposite effect had happened and, in the chaos and desperation of those attempting to gain entry, the surge of bodies had created a fatal crush. Seven people died. They were either trampled, suffocated, or suffered a heart attack.

We already knew about it before it became news. Members of the Nowzad team had informed us in a meeting. I had spoken on BBC News just days earlier to state that if the system for entry was not completely revisited and new procedures weren't put in place, then people would die. I wasn't happy to have been proven right.

I closed my eyes as I once again tried to fathom how I was going to work a miracle and drive two trucks loaded high with dogs and cats followed by two buses containing sixty-odd Afghan nationals – mostly children and women, including two several months along in their pregnancies – into the airport when people were currently dying while attempting to do the same.

On the 22nd of August the Associated Press website ran a story by Ahmad Seir, Tameem Akhgar, and Jon Gambrell about it. The kicker of the AP article was this paragraph:

> "Biden told reporters at the White House that 11,000 people had been airlifted from Kabul in a 36-hour period this weekend, although he did not provide details. The number appeared to include flights by charter and non-U.S. military

aircraft as well as the U.S. Air Force C-17 and C-130 transport planes that have been flying daily from the capital."

The words rang round my head. "The number appeared to include flights by charter and non-US military aircraft". The article just confirmed what I had been hearing from friends within American military circles who had hinted that influential groups in the US were sending aircraft to rescue their particular interests in Afghanistan.

Yet numerous British government ministers had been turning up on British news channels to tell the British public that our chartered flight would mess up the military evacuation, although the arrival of chartered flights did not seem a problem for the US.

We were well and truly being taken for a ride by the British government.

All we needed was a slot for one chartered aircraft, at no cost to the British taxpayer, to land on an airfield that was already catering to non-military aircraft. I couldn't see the issue. I was just so despondent. I felt helpless.

But there was one thing I could do. I could at least get the lorries we needed and line everything up so that we were all ready to go, should the British government ever grant us permission.

–

"You ready?" I was apprehensive. The guys seemed confident in the plan. I had no moving part to play. I just had to hide. Simple really.

Nina had managed somehow to resource a reliable Hawala provider, or to give them their proper title, a Hawaladar.

Based in Dubai and with references that had checked out, he promised Nina that the money would be in Kabul within twenty-four hours of the transaction commencing.

And true to his word, Farid received a call to say the courier was on route to our clinic, with our desperately needed $80,000 in cash.

Our next immediate concern had been that whilst we trusted the Hawaladar as much as we could, the courier was an unknown. We reckoned it would not be beyond the realms of possibility that for a back-hander, he could drop the money with us whilst also having tipped off a criminal gang. The fact that our compound was about to have $80,000 in cash stashed within it was not something I took lightly. Having our compound invaded by a cash-hungry gang was not on my to-do list anytime soon. Even though I was armed, home invasions don't often end well.

With Kabul's police force now defunct, criminality was on the rise as the Taliban took their time to consolidate their presence within the capital.

So we decided to stage a play.

The scene was set. It was a simple ruse but one we hoped would deter any gang looking to make a quick buck. The courier would be shown into the compound and led through to the office. Farid and Mujtaba would be waiting for him. The courier would be kept standing whilst Farid made a big show of counting the money and then placing it in a large brown envelope.

Ensuring the courier heard the next conversation was crucial as Farid would stand up and hand the envelope to Mujtaba along with the lines of, "Get this to Amir now to buy the lorries, before he sells them to someone else."

Mujtaba was to take the package and leave the office at a run. Whilst Farid engaged the courier in small talk, I would be waiting, hidden away in the garden with another brown envelope stuffed with blank paper. An exchange would take place. Mujtaba would then leave the compound at pace, turning and disappearing down Shura Street, brown envelope firmly under his arm, just in case the criminal gang had employed a spotter to watch the compound. The courier would later corroborate that the cash had indeed left our compound. Mujtaba was under strict instructions not to return to the compound for at least an hour and to ditch the stuffed envelope in a drainage ditch well away from prying eyes.

Meanwhile, I would sneak around the back of the house to my office carrying the $80,000 in cash in the original envelope.

When the time came, the ruse worked like a charm. Our BAFTA was assured. Mujtaba apparently sat and drank tea in a street café on the other side of the park for an hour before taking a gentle stroll back to the clinic. Whilst he was gone, Farid and I counted the cash, dividing it into the necessary payments we had to make. We commenced by paying the staff their salaries and buying some much-needed hay for the donkey sanctuary.

Farid and Aman, our night-time security guard, handled the purchase of the lorries, which at first glance seemed like they had seen better days. Aman gunned the engines to show me they worked just fine. And as Farid reminded me, it was a one-way trip.

To curtail any suspicion by the neighbours or indeed the Taliban now holed up in the fire station, Farid thought it best if we parked the trucks away from the Nowzad compound. I agreed with him. We would only bring them to the front to be loaded a few minutes before we were ready for that phase of the plan.

The arrival of the cash had been a weight lifted, but the relief was only momentary. One box had been ticked but too many others were still pending.

Mujtaba sat at his desk in the now-sparse office all day, continually pouring over spreadsheets containing health and vaccination data relating to the 171 animals we would be taking with us. Microchip numbers are notoriously long, fifteen numbers to be precise and if just one digit is found not to match on any of the many required forms, then the compulsory six-month quarantine could run into thousands of pounds or, the scenario we all feared, the animal would be put to sleep by the authorities.

His phone was on speed dial to Jen, perched in front of her desk in southern England, and the control centre for the mass import. And it wasn't just the one set of matching paperwork which was required to be completed 171 times. Oh no, each of the four different quarantine facilities we were using all had their own variations.

It was, to be honest, an epic. As we drifted in limbo towards the end of August, our evac committee meetings were becoming more and more desperate.

I always started the day with a trip around the Zoom screen to get the updates in from the team.

"Hi Nina, how are we with the aircraft landing slot?" I would ask hoping for some positive news.

"Sorry Pen, no closer. But I hope to have some good news tomorrow," she would say helpfully.

I'd then turn to look at Sam and Trudy. "How is the permission for the staff?"

You're going to hear about Trudy later but in short, Trudy Harrison, Member of Parliament for Copeland and Parliamentary Private Secretary to the Prime Minister, was a volunteer with our evac team. This sounds like we had a direct line to the PM. Obviously, we didn't.

"Hi Pen," Sam would answer on behalf of both of them. "All the paperwork has been submitted but we are waiting on FDCO to confirm."

I moved onto the next screen.

"Ok, Jen, please give me some good news on the import licenses for the dogs and cats!" Although I had an idea what the reply would be.

"Well Pen, sixteen animals don't need quarantine, which include Ragnar and Cora," she said, smiling. Technically I had known that already but smiled back anyway. "But we are still waiting for APHA/DEFRA to issue the 171 licenses that we need."

I looked down at the desk to the list of permissions left unchecked that were required to pull Operation Ark off. "David, how about the aircraft? Have we secured one yet even if it can't land?" I winked in Nina's direction, failing to remember that everybody on the Zoom call would have thought I was winking at them.

"I have some leads from a group chat on LinkedIn," he replied. "It's the insurance that is the issue. Lloyd's of London won't issue the bond for anyone to land in Kabul."

I smiled at everyone on the call. "Great meeting, team," I said sarcastically. "Same time tomorrow?"

We all laughed but out of frustration. Everyone on the

call knew it was the 22nd of August. The countdown until the Americans pulled the plug on the evacuation was eight days away at most.

We were running out of time.

24 August 2021

I needed something to do that wasn't Operation Ark. The 9pm news in the UK was 1am for me in Kabul, and the Los Angeles afternoon TV show was interviewing me at 5am.

I changed into my gym stuff, put my thoroughly sweat-stained shirt and cargo pants through the washing machine, and beasted myself through a twenty-minute workout followed by a cold shower. My last protein bar and a steaming hot cup of breakfast tea later, I was back in the game feeling just slightly refreshed.

Our only success of the last few days was that Jen had finally secured the licenses for all 171 animals to arrive in the United Kingdom. It was truly a huge credit to her, Tom, and Mujtaba for their hard work in making it happen.

But it was, of course, useless without an aircraft to transport them in. We had no aircraft because we had no permission from the British government to land one. We were no closer to receiving permission to land a chartered aircraft than we had been on the 14th of August. And I saw no reason why anything would change.

I thought about it long and hard. It was hopeless. The decision had been made for me.

On the evening of the 24th of August I called time on Operation Ark. I summoned the evacuation team for what I thought would be our final team Zoom call.

We had failed.

The mood was sombre. Depressing.

Sod this. "Find alcohol. We are having a party to celebrate all that we have achieved."

I beamed to the assembled faces on the screen. And to be

fair we had made waves. A group of just four people at the start of the withdrawal had turned into a steadfast group who had rallied hundreds of thousands of people around the world to our cause, raising over a million pounds. But we had gone up against a government who, it seemed, had other ideas.

I returned to my desk with my Yeti filled to the brim with red wine. I estimated I could fill another mug and then that was it. I was on the wagon.

It was already nearly midnight. The Zoom call mood picked up quickly with the addition of alcohol and music. We chatted and laughed about everything other than what would happen tomorrow to me, the staff, and our animals. I knew I was staying. I tried not to think about it. Wine helped.

Kaisa and her dad joined from Norway. Dan rang in from his office in Texas. The British evac team joined from their various homes around the UK. Trudy joined from her home office up north, cracking open a bottle of wine and toasting our efforts.

After an hour or so I needed a top-up. I made my excuse to the call and left them chatting as I took the opportunity to use the bathroom and then nip downstairs to my bedroom to refill my Yeti.

As they say in the Marines, like a lightweight I failed to return to the Zoom party. The call went on without me until the early hours of the UK when the last of the team realised they were talking to themselves.

All of us had been in a wine-induced sleep when Ben Wallace, the British Defence Secretary in charge of the evacuation who had been highly vocal about his displeasure at what I was trying to achieve with Operation Ark, posted a late-night tweet.

At 0133hrs (UK Local) on the 25th of August, Wallace tweeted,

> "Now that Pen Farthing's staff have been cleared to come forward under LOTR I have authorised MOD to facilitate their processing alongside all other eligible personnel at HKIA. At that stage, if he arrives with his animals we will seek a slot for his plane."

I was gobsmacked. The day before Wallace had yelled "Bollocks!" on the live LBC radio show with Nick Ferrari. Nick had read aloud one of my tweets about the staff and animals being abandoned, and Wallace had lost it. Then he'd ranted a bit. LBC asked for me to comment. Quite genuinely I told them I was surprised at Wallace's language. Both Nick Ferrari and I had a chuckle about it.

And how insane was it that we were being informed via tweet?

Whatever. We had finally been given permission for Operation Ark to become a reality.

Kaisa's father, Rune, was the first to see the tweet. He excitedly woke up Kaisa who, upon not being able to wake me, called Nina. Nina called Mujtaba who was about to start his morning prayers. Banging loudly on my bedroom door, he shouted out my name. "Pen, Pen, wake up!" But I was out cold.

Mujtaba opened the door, peeking in. It was a sight he won't forget in a hurry.

There I was flat out on my bed, fully dressed, my empty Yeti cup clasped in my right hand but resting on my chest, snoring away with the best of them. Clearly, I had sat on the edge of the bed, full of good intentions to fill the Yeti, but had instead passed out.

As I groggily opened my eyes to assess what was happening, Mujtaba handed me the phone. "It's Nina," he said, a big smile on his face. He already knew what she was going to tell me.

Nina's voice was pure joy. "Pen!" she screamed down the phone. "It's happening. Wallace has given us permission!"

It was Nina who then told a slightly worse-for-wear Trudy, that it was a go. Trudy had only just woken up herself and not heard anything through official channels. Trudy's reaction in our group, and I quote, was:

"WTF – I finished the bottle, cried buckets, only just woke up and think I might be delirious – is this really real?"

–

We did not to know this at the time, but the permission given in the crazy-early hours (UK Local) of the 25th would leave us just forty-eight hours to roll our way into the airport before the Brits collapsed the cordon. Their final act in Afghanistan would be to concentrate on evacuating the 16th Air Assault assets on the 28th of August, bringing to an end twenty years of British boots on the ground.

I forget the number of people who thought we had an aircraft sitting on standby in an adjacent country, burning and turning on the runway, waiting for my "go". An aircraft that they thought could have been used to aid the evacuation whilst it waited to collect me.

We didn't and it couldn't. Firstly, we only had enough funding for our chartered aircraft to fly in, collect us, and drop us somewhere safe. And secondly, we had to give the broker a specific date and time. Two major factors I had not the slightest clue about. If it was not so mind-bogglingly serious, I would have laughed.

I sat upright on my bed. I was still more than tired and now, for added fun, I had a headache.

25 August 2021

The morning was chaos. Utter chaos. I called a staff meeting of the heads of the families who were currently residing in the house. Najwa's old family room she had shared with Mirwais and Ibrahim now housed two families. Our living room was home to another two families. The guest room had been the refuge for our single female staff for the last week but now, along with the safe room, was occupied by family members from one of the teams.

A few of the team had insisted on keeping their families at their homes, dotted across Kabul.

"Now is the time to bring everyone in," I said in English to the assembled faces, all eager for news yet dreading the journey we were about to embark on. Mujtaba translated for me. I saw smiles break out around the gathering.

"We have been given permission to take you all to the United Kingdom." I smiled like a Cheshire cat as I said it. Everyone immediately started clapping and chatting excitedly.

"Yak Daka!" I shouted happily. "One minute. We have to get there first," I reminded them before they became too complacent.

Their smiles never wavered as Mujtaba translated the rest of the meeting for me, while I detailed timings and reminded them of the need to pack light. I had ordered a full search of everyone's belongings in three hours, a sort of a pre-flight baggage check. I was keen to ensure none of the Nowzad staff or their families were caught out by attempting to take any contraband out of the country.

We finalised the meal timings for the sixty-odd people living under the Nowzad roof and set about preparing a meal for the cats and dogs. If all went to plan, I had no idea when either the staff or animals would next eat.

Morning turned to afternoon as the day dragged on. It was beyond hot. My shirt was constantly stuck to my back and sweat ran down my face as I double-checked every aspect of our move. Mujtaba was buried in what seemed like two piles of highly stacked paper as he finished yet another phone call with Jen.

As the day progressed, our evacuation meeting brought us no closer leaving the compound as two major flaws had come to the fore.

Worryingly, Nina and David seemed no closer to confirming we had an aircraft, as we still had no idea who from the British government we were meant to be discussing the details with. Even though Wallace had tweeted that we had permission, still nothing official had been sent out to us. Trudy promised to chase it, but like us, she was unsure who to contact as she wasn't sure who had given us permission. Think about that – there was such a complete lack of leadership within the government that the PM's Private Secretary didn't know who had given us authorisation.

I needed to clear my head and took the opportunity to go and play with Ragnar and Cora. Tail wags went into overdrive as I undid the latch on the gate and slipped inside before the other occupants they shared the kennel enclosure with could Steve McQueen it. I rubbed ears and bellies as wriggly dogs jumped and squirmed for my affections. I plonked my arse on the dusty ground as a tongue cleaned out my left ear for me. "Cheers, Cora." I beamed and closed my mouth quickly before I ended up with Ragnar French-kissing me. He settled instead on licking the right side of my face.

Again the thought of not getting them out of Afghanistan flashed through my brain. What was I going to do if I couldn't? Just release them? They had never fended for themselves. They had been with me since pups.

If nothing came of today then I was seriously in stay-behind territory, to ride out whatever was going to happen so that I could be here for those who needed me the most. And I had no idea what that was going to be. The Taliban was reasserting its authority over the country, but if I couldn't get our people and animals out, then I was going to be here to at least try and steer a course through whatever came next for Afghanistan. I had no idea if that was brave or just stupid of me.

Finally, at 13.59hrs (Kabul Local) my email inbox pinged with an email headed "IMPORTANT".

REF: L/SPC/042

To: Paul Pen Farthing

You are being evacuated to the United Kingdom by the British Military.

You must go to the Baron Hotel, Zohak Village, Kabul today. You must bring all your passports. Do not tell anyone where you are going.

Expect a long wait – please bring water and food with you. Travel safely and carefully, use your own judgement, do not put yourself at unnecessary risk. If you cannot arrive by today, continue to the Baron Hotel, we will evacuate you after you arrive.

Each person may bring 1 x 9kg bag only – do not bring more.

Print this email as proof of authorisation for Leave Outside Usual Rules.

The sheer unhelpfulness of the email wound me up. It demonstrated a complete lack of understanding of the reality of the situation. They *were* evacuating me to the United Kingdom, but only if I managed to gain access to the airport surrounded by the Taliban and crowds of desperate people. Carrying this letter did not give me unheeded access to the Baron Hotel, as proved by Najwa and Kaisa's ill-fated first attempt to leave back on the 17th of August.

And I had to do it by the end of today apparently, yet they hadn't sent the email to me until 13.59 (Kabul Local). Two o'clock in the afternoon. Even if I had been on my own, it was not like I could just walk out of the compound and hail a taxi.

As the only permission I had was my own, that put paid to any sudden urgency in departing. Operation Ark included the staff being evacuated. And with most of them not computer literate, their permission emails were destined to come to me.

For the next two-and-a-bit hours my email would occasionally ping as I received another email granting permission for another of our staff. It was nail-bitingly tense.

At 4.09pm, Salim, who had artfully dodged the Taliban a few days before whilst overloaded with naan, received his email. He was the last. That was everybody.

This was it. We were leaving.

But it didn't exactly leave us a whole lot of time to get our circus on the move. As the last document I thought I'd ever print on the Nowzad printer slid out, I yelled for Farid.

Now all we needed was a lift. I rang Nina to find out any word on whether we had an aircraft.

As the sun began its slow descending arc behind the harsh square edges of the Nowzad clinic, I stood on the balcony that backed out of the guest bedroom for one last time. Secretly, I was longing for the coolness the early evening sans sun would bring.

The railings surrounding the three sides of the balcony were adorned with hessian green screen. It was usually found as a tactical aid fastened to the chain link fencing that surrounded military bases, limiting what could be witnessed inside the wire. The shielding made the balcony a complete sun trap. And Kaisa loved to sunbathe. Mostly not wearing a lot. The screen earnt the effort it took in fixing it around the balcony.

I closed my eyes as I felt the last of the early evening sun against my face, the images of moments now lost in history playing one last time as a film reel through my brain.

On my last birthday, Kaisa and I turned the balcony into an outdoor pool with the assistance of a blow-up paddling pool we'd found in a shop in the centre of Kabul. We had carefully carried the large TV from the living room onto the balcony, balanced ever so delicately on top of, what I assumed, was a sturdy plastic table. A connecting HDMI cable from my laptop (with full disregard for electrics being in such proximity to a paddling pool full of water) meant we had our Zoom screen as large as life in front of us. Family and friends from around the world had joined for my birthday celebration as Kaisa and I sat in the pool of warm water, drank a few beers, and laughed lots. It had been a bloody good day.

As I walked onto the balcony now, I noted our old original handwoven Afghan rug, its hue and colours making it a true work of art, rolled up carefully and placed on the floor next to my bed. It hadn't been moved in months. The carpet had appeared one day at the Nowzad clinic, and to this day I have no idea where it came from. Always an admirer of its elegance and beauty, I had hoped I would one day "acquire" it, somehow facilitating its journey back to England.

The sight of the carpet caused my mind to race back to a harshly cold February night when Kaisa and I had snuggled up upon that very carpet, propped up against a mountain of Afghan pillows. The night sky had obliged us with shooting star displays that made us exclaim, one of us proudly pointing out the sparkling satellite streaking across the night sky before the other had chance to call it.

The Kabul skyline in all directions was dotted with many small rock faces and cliffs that would have been a first ascensionist's dream. Fridays would have been ideal for an adventure amongst those unclimbed rocks – if only stranger-averse locals and the failing security conditions would have allowed it. Instead, I'd surprised Kaisa with a climbing adventure that never even left our compound.

With our climbing rope and gear I'd led an intrigued Kaisa through a merry dance of climbing and swinging from branch to mostly stable branch through the trees that lined the side of the main house, until one delicate little step from a creaking branch had brought us both to the uncertain safety of the corrugated roof of the house. Attaching a rope around the chimney stack allowed us to swing our legs out over the edge of the roof, dangling above the thirty-foot drop to the patio below.

Still hidden from view by the tightly woven leaf-covered tree branches, I'd opened my rucksack to retrieve the bottle of champagne I'd bought from duty-free in Dubai on my last trip out. We'd sat as carefree as two little birds, sipping champagne from travel cups as the world carried on without us.

As I looked around the balcony now, the memories threatened to overwhelm my tired mind. Then I was chuckling at another memory: Basir falling off the roof whilst completely engrossed with his kite flying. We'd all thought he was dead. But being Afghan, he was made of sterner stuff and just rolled over, laughing.

I stood silently as the darkening shadows in the compound grew longer. The memories were overwhelming. The now-familiar anger, hurt, and sadness returned. Our charity was losing everything we had built. And worst of all, the people of Afghanistan were losing their future. The tears came in a wave. I stood motionless, unable to move as the last light of the sun fully sunk behind the clinic.

The buried Royal Marine inside of me battled fiercely to clamber through the emotional turmoil and take up the reins.

"Ignore and override," I said to no one. It was time to get my game head back on and get everyone, our people *and* animals, to safety. I had to focus. I was charged with getting the families, including young children, safely into that airport. I turned on my heel and strode away from the balcony I would never set foot on again.

I was now Kurt Russell's Snake Plissken, but this wasn't New York, it was Kabul.

When I had announced that today was D-Day, that we were leaving, it had taken nearly six frantic hours to put everything in place for our departure. The remaining team members' families had gathered at the compound, the baggage inspection had been conducted and the searched bags were now under lock and key. Everything was set.

Then I'd called a final meeting with the head of each family and our vet team. Everybody sat anxiously in the Nowzad office. It was the last briefing I would ever give there. Perched on the edge of a coffee table, I started.

Tick-tock, tick-tock as we crept slowly towards H-Hour, the moment we would leave the compound. Consultation with the evac committee had determined that we leave in the dead of night for the journey to the airport.

After giving a final brief to everyone on their roles and our "actions-on" in the event everything went pear-shaped, I looked around the blank faces staring back at me. None of us in that room had any idea what was about to happen. Inwardly, I was extremely anxious of what was to come, but I did my best not to show it. Everyone seemed to be looking to me for guidance. With no more questions that needed to be answered, I smiled and said, "Rosa Hosh," aka, "Happy Days."

Grins broke out on the faces of the gathered group. I glanced at my watch. It was 2200hrs (Kabul Local). Time to pull the pin.

I clapped my hands and shouted "Englishstan." Dari for England.

With that, the Nowzad crew set about a very carefully planned timetable of events to ensure we were ready for our departure time of 2300hrs. Each member of the vet team had a designated task. Mujtaba was in overall charge of the loading plan for getting the dogs and cats into crates, while Farid was charged with ensuring the occupied crates were stacked, ready to be loaded into the relevant lorry so we could offload them quicky once in the airport. Hamida took charge of the cats in the cat room and clinic. Zahra the First oversaw organising the families. Every member had a piece of orange tape secured around their arm so we could clearly identify everyone should we have to abandon the buses and become separated amongst the crowds that had formed around the gates. The men were tasked with the manual labour of loading the two trucks.

Yet everything had to be done silently.

The house next door to us was owned by a money launderer. We deduced that from the amount of people that arrived in the dead of night weighed down with huge bags but left empty-handed. We'd watched these events on our CCTV cameras as they were trained across the main vehicle entrance to the clinic and our home.

And he hated dogs. We knew that from his many visits to see Farid to complain about the dog noise. Farid had also clocked very early on he was pro-Taliban. Not a good combination, especially now with the Taliban detachment who had taken up residency in the fire station across the road.

The outside hard standing of the clinic soon became cluttered with travel crates of all sizes and colours as dogs were loaded according to the carefully arranged plan. Everywhere I looked there were crates, either waiting to be filled or now cable-tied shut. From some crates two little wet noses poked out between the bars. I felt guilty for cramming two dogs inside a crate designed for one, but then again, I had no choice if I wanted to save as many as I could. The discomfort would be short-lived, I hoped. Staff members were busy bringing dogs to the designated load area, to have their microchips scanned by Mujtaba before he assigned them to their respective travel crate.

Once secured, their crate would be lifted and carried off to the waiting trucks parked outside.

I stole a quick glance inside the clinic, which was another scene of manic activity as Fazad, Zahra the Second, and Hamida fussed around crates stacked on every available flat surface. Cats meowed as they were removed from their cages and placed inside their travel crate.

The whole thing was a slick operation, meticulously planned and carried out by the staff. I was incredibly proud of them. I had faith we could pull this off.

Dr Reshad was staying. Bright and just the nicest person you could wish to meet, he was heavily invested in bettering himself for the promotion of animal welfare. His extended family had asked him to stay and not be part of Operation Ark. He had listened to their wishes and so was remaining behind. Whilst I was sad he was not going to be starting a new life in England, I was also relieved that it would be him looking after our donkey sanctuary. If anyone could keep it running whilst the Taliban began their rule, it was Dr Reshad.

As the families filed silently on to their designated bus, I took a moment to say goodbye properly to Dr Reshad.

We shook hands and then hugged. "Keep safe, my friend," was all I could offer him.

He nodded and responded in kind, "You too, Sir."

I watched as Aman hugged his brother. Male family

relatives had volunteered to come in and help Dr Reshad close the clinic once we left. Aman was unlikely to see his brother ever again, such was the magnitude of our evacuation from Afghanistan. It was the price he had chosen to give his young family a new start in the United Kingdom, thousands of miles away from the Taliban.

The very filthy interior of the lorry cab was designed for two people, at most. But we were three not-so-averagely-built people. Farid was driving, I was squeezed in the middle, and Dr Mujtaba was to my right. The jarring from every bump and corner turn didn't help one bit.

I had worked through a hundred scenarios for what to do in the event that we were stopped and I was taken hostage by the Taliban. I chuckled inside my head as I thought about the options. "Cheerfulness under adversity," as Trudy liked to remind me during our Zoom meetings.

> Fight to the death – always a good option for the hero fraternity.
> Fight and run – simple and effective if you can.
> Just run – good if you are wearing running shoes and have no baggage. I had two lorries and two buses.
> Play the British passport card and hope for the best.

And the last option was exactly what I did.

We had travelled exactly 300 metres from the Nowzad compound when a Taliban fighter stepped out from the shadows behind a concrete checkpoint belonging to the old Ministry of Business.

He pointed his AK-47 rifle directly at the cab of the truck Mujtaba, Farid, and I were occupying.

As we pulled to a stop, more Talibs stepped from the darkness of the unlit ministry. All were pointing their weapons.

As we parked, I sent a quick message to Hamida, so she knew what was happening up front, and so would disseminate to the other vehicles the same message. It simply read "Taliban – stay in vehicle."

All three of us, without consulting each other, raised our hands in a slow-motion surrender. We were staring down the barrels of a dozen guns.

Most of the Talibs were young and the automatic weapons they now pointed at us had probably been thrust into their hands with little basic training.

And one of them proved it. His finger on the trigger, safety catch not applied, must have involuntarily squeezed. Thankfully, his rifle was set to single shot and not automatic.

The bullet from the end of his rifle sailed over the top of the convoy. If he had been pointing it directly at us in that moment, one of us would not be here right now.

It was also the only time I ever heard Farid swear in English.

"Fuck."

I could not have agreed with him more. We watched as the young Talib squirmed in embarrassment while his fellow fighters berated him.

I realised I had been holding my breath. I let out a long "Phew."

For nearly thirty minutes we sat there, open palms raised forward. All three of us watched as more Taliban arrived in multiple pickup trucks. We tallied forty-two who now surrounded our four vehicles. Every single one of them carried an automatic weapon.

None approached us until finally a pickup truck arrived to deposit the commander – a fairly rotund individual with a thick beard and pure white turban that ended with a long flowing piece of cloth.

He proceeded to approach the vehicle accompanied by his heavily armed security detail. Farid opened the door to the truck slowly. They spoke briefly, all jovial and not as intimidating as I had expected.

The commander pointed to me. "American?" he asked.

I vehemently shook my head in reply. "No, no. British." I held up my passport.

He motioned for Farid to pass it to him. For the next thirty minutes we waited, the three of us staring through the windscreen of the cab as the leadership of the Taliban checkpoint literally sat down in the middle of the Shura Street and held a shura deciding what to do with us.

Their decision still amazes me to this day. The commander returned with my passport.

"We will escort you," he said all matter-of-factly. "The airport gate is closed but you can enter in the morning."

And with that our humanitarian convoy was escorted by four white Toyota pickup trucks, hazard lights flashing, crammed full of heavily armed men, in the direction of the airport. Farid, Mujtaba, and I just sat smiling the whole way.

–

I finished circling our four-vehicle convoy. The darkness of the street where we parked was impenetrable. Nothing stirred. No cars cruised down this stretch of tarmacked road.

And the heat was still overwhelming even at three o'clock in the morning. Once again my cotton Nowzad insignia-decorated shirt clung to me. And it stank. Each bus had all the side windows wide open in a fruitless attempt to allow cool air to circulate the confines of the cramped interior. The snag was, there was no cool air. As I peered in the open door of both buses, families huddled against each other. Others slept on the floor in between the seats. Nobody looked comfortable.

Not sounding that far away, the occasional *rat tat tat* sound of gunfire along with one-off thuds of what I assumed were flashbangs, a small non-lethal explosive device designed to stun your senses rather than kill or maim you, echoed down the road, breaking the eerie quiet of the night. I guessed these tactics were being used in a clumsy attempt to disperse people from scrambling their way toward the Abbey Gate entrance.

If I listened intently whilst stood next to the trucks, there wasn't a sound except, now and again, the creaking noise of a crate shifting as a dog or cat attempted to find a more comfortable spot. Sometimes a muffled growl emerged from deep within the tightly stacked truck beds as one dog encroached on its buddy's personal space within the cramped confines.

"Shhh," I would say quietly in the vague direction the growl had emanated. I realised it was pointless but doing nothing at all to try and reassure the dogs seemed lame.

I tried not to think about the conditions inside those tightly stacked travel crates. Any ice in their water bowls would have melted long ago. Anything that hadn't been drunk would have spilt onto the floor of the plastic kennel while we'd bounced and lurched from side to side as we drove along Kabul's less-than-well-maintained roads. And a stagnant mixture of cat and dog wee probably added to the mix.

Not a damn thing I could do about it now. Even attempting to clean one of the dog crates would result in a crescendo of barking and howling.

I turned away from the back of the tarp-covered truck and nodded in the direction of two posted sentries. Zakia's teenage sons were stood upright against one of the many trees that lined the road on the opposite side of the deep drainage ditch. The two of them were quietly surveying the scene and chatting amongst themselves. They nodded back.

I had decided to run a two-hour rotating sentry routine just in case any inquisitive folk unable to sleep and out for a midnight stroll decided to see what we were keeping under our tarps. In that event, then the male Afghan members of our team were tasked with intervening.

I was on red alert. Every fibre of my body was tensed. "Just like a striking cobra," as we were partial to say once upon a time in the Marines. I laughed quietly as I thought it. We were so full of shit back in the day.

But I was ready to react to the slightest thing that didn't seem right. Twenty-odd years of serving in the toughest fighting unit of the United Kingdom's military had taught me not be complacent. Always expect the unexpected. And then be ready to deal with it.

We were so vulnerable parked where we were, lined up along the curb of what was known as the forty-metre road. The south entrance to Kabul airport was just 400 metres away at the first exit of the airport "circle" or, to us Brits, the airport roundabout. The second exit, straight across the roundabout, was a claustrophobic channelled road that led to the now-infamous Abbey Gate.

The third exit led towards the US embassy and Massoud Circle with the centrepiece a huge column that was dedicated to Afghan's Ahmad Shah Massoud, the hero of the fight against the Taliban.

Those were my choices. Every man and his dog thought I was going for the Baron Hotel and then the Abbey Gate.

But I wasn't.

I knew the Abbey Gate entrance like the back of my hand. I had honestly forgotten how many times I had been there. Just a month earlier Kaisa and I, accompanied by Cora had travelled there.

Our journey was to meet with Michael, an American soldier who had originally taken it upon himself to care for a little white puppy he had stumbled across one day whilst he was based at Camp Morehead, home of the Afghan Commandos. Michael had been just one of a handful of United States soldiers in post to train the commandos. The camp was run by the book and a strict "no stray dog" policy meant the little pup he cared for would suffer an excruciating end at the hands of the Afghan army if she was found.

With porous fencing surrounding the remote base, strays would wander in to scavenge amongst the discarded rubbish, often coming across generous pickings compared to what was on offer in the surrounding local villages. Sadly, every few months or so, the local Afghan commander would order a purge and any strays unfortunate enough to be on the hunt for food that day would find an abundance of poisoned meat.

Michael had cared for the little playful pup as long as he could until she became too big to continue to hide in his quarters. She had begun to adopt the traits that everybody who cares for an Afghan dog will recognise immediately. She became protective of her perceived family and would bark whenever she felt they were threatened. And that was every time she saw an Afghan soldier approaching. Which was just bad news when the camp was full of Afghan soldiers.

Michael knew of Nowzad. We had supported some of his colleagues who had adopted strays whilst serving at Camp Morehead previously. As soon as Michael had called us, we'd driven out of Kabul proper and headed southeast to meet him along mostly-deserted potholed roads to rendezvous at the remote camp entrance for the handover.

I always revelled in the surprised look I would receive as a fully tooled-up soldier realised that I'd driven out into the sticks with just Mirwais to accompany me in what was very clearly an unarmoured vehicle. But our lack of military equipment and support had allowed us to just blend into the natural ebb and flow of life outside of Kabul. Nobody ever stopped us.

"You came in just that?" Michael had asked incredulously, peering out from behind his Oakley-issued sunglasses in the direction of our battered van.

"She does the job, mate," I'd replied smiling as I extended my hand. "Nice to meet you in person finally."

We'd shaken hands and Michael immediately began to hand over supplies and treats he had collected for Cora before finally turning and picking up the travel crate with its precious cargo. No soldier wanted to be exposed for any period at the entrance to a military camp, a sentiment shared by both Mirwais and I.

We'd both accepted that this was our moment of greatest risk during any rescue operation, not because we thought we would be vulnerable to being attacked, but due to the very real threat of being identified and then followed.

I'd carefully taken the crate from Michael and peered inside. A wet nose had pressed against the wire gate of the crate to investigate the new guy.

"Hello there, little one," I'd enthused as I let her sniff my fingers. "You'll be safe with us."

"Keep safe," Michael had yelled as we saddled up in the van.

I'd leant out of the passenger window as Mirwais deftly turned the van in the restrictive approach to the gate and yelled back, "Keep your head down too, mate." Camp Morehead was soon fading from our review mirrors as we travelled along the bumpy roads on the return journey to the Nowzad clinic and Cora's new home.

Now Michael was finishing his tour and had been recalled to the Baron Hotel whilst he waited for his flight home. We'd brought Cora along so he could say goodbye to the pup he had saved before he left Afghanistan for good.

So yes, I knew the road well.

With everything being quiet, I intended to get some shut-eye. I climbed to a perch atop the lead cab using the sturdy wing mirror as a foot placement. It was the first climbing I had done in a long time. I smiled at the thought. I could not wait for this to be over so my long-planned retirement in Norway alongside Kaisa could begin in earnest.

I fell into a restless sleep, totally unaware of the shitstorm that the new day would bring.

26 August 2021

"Alright, mate."

I was slightly taken aback. The north London accent threw me. Fully dressed in the traditional Islamic shalwar kameez and sporting a full beard, the accent of the Afghan gentleman directly in front of me seemed out of place.

"Mohammad," he offered as I shook the outstretched hand. "You're that Dog Guy?"

Busted. Our low profile as we waited in the shadow of the trees was about to become high profile.

Mohammad was a bus driver from London. He showed me his British passport as proof. His wife and three children were sat further down the road against a tree. In Kabul to visit family, the Taliban's arrival had thrown his travel back to the UK into disarray. Firsthand he'd witnessed the carnage at the Abbey Gate and was not about to risk his family's safety by attempting entry that way. And he wasn't alone. He knew of another five or six family groups, all British passport holders, camped out along this road waiting as well. None were willing to risk the Abbey Gate.

We made small talk for a few minutes. Not once did he voice displeasure at what I was attempting. We wished each other well in our attempts at getting home. I was lucky – Nowzad had supporters in England who were pushing Defence Secretary Ben Wallace and the British government to get me, the animals, and the staff out. These other British citizens did not. The BBC reported on the 27th of August that around 150 Britons had been left behind.

The gate had remained closed most of the day. Mujtaba and I walked the 400 metres, often through densely packed crowds, to reach the barricaded main south entrance to the airport. Upside down baggage trolleys had been used by the Taliban to build a defensive line and several Talibs sporting large bamboo batons as deterrents ensured that nobody attempted to cross that line.

"When is it going to open?" Mujtaba asked the nearest Talib, ensuring he stayed a safe distance away so he wouldn't be mistaken for attempting to breach the line and therefore beaten.

"When the commander wills it," was the simple reply. He did not seem a happy chap and we had no desire to provoke him. He, after all, was the one with a big stick and an AK-47 slung over his shoulder.

None the wiser we walked back, stopping once to make use of the washroom facilities offered by the local mosque to all those waiting patiently along its walls.

The heat was debilitating. Farid had purchased water for everyone along with fresh naan bread from one of the many bakers carrying out a roaring trade along this stretch of the road. Basir, Hamida, and the two Zahras had fashioned squirty water bottles, and were doing what they could to get water into as many mouths as possible from the crates that were accessible.

The day continued like that until the Talib commander from the previous evening's encounter arrived at roughly four o'clock in the afternoon. He spoke to Farid and before I knew what was really happening, we were a convoy again. Farid, Mujtaba, and I crammed into the lead truck as all four vehicles pulled out into the middle of the road, led by a Talib commander in a Toyota pickup.

And that was how we were able to drive into the south

gate of Kabul Airport. Because a Taliban commander – not a single member of the British military – led us through the various outer ring checkpoints.

I sat rather smugly as everything seemed to be going better than I could have ever hoped for. "We are in!" I exclaimed to Mujtaba and Farid, even high-fiving both as we crossed under the curving sign that spanned the entrance gate and displayed "Kabul Airport" in huge letters.

We had done it.

The elation and self-congratulatory attitude lasted all of two minutes. After travelling 300 yards along the terminal approach road, our rather friendly escort handed us over to a new commander. And this new commander had very different ideas about our planned evacuation.

–

At 11.02am, (UK Local), Nina created yet another WhatsApp chat group with all the familiar faces, to facilitate the move into the airport proper.

The text messages are copied exactly (so please excuse spelling) with timings, all UK local. My notes are in *italics*.

[26/08/2021, 11:02:00] EXIT: Nina created group "EXIT"

[26/08/2021, 11:03:02] Nina: Ok - thing I've explained to most we must get back on this as a group. Comms are otherwise getting lost. I suggest we keep it brief and valid, and then branch off if required for the finer details.

[26/08/2021, 11:03:24] Nina: David - can you just write here exactly what's going on with our flight pls? Which bit is now off the table. Thanks

[26/08/2021, 11:04:15] Ian: yep. re comms that press release by Sam a good place to start, but let's sort flight details

[26/08/2021, 11:15:22] Ian: right so it's nothing to do with us. USA hogging all the flights UK pushed to back of queue. only USA can get Pen in there. or Wallace ringing US Defence sec

[26/08/2021, 11:18:54] Dora the Explorer: Just checking… Should Pen be on this chat?

I still laugh and shake my head in mild disbelief that I wasn't the first person to be added to the group.

[26/08/2021, 11:19:16] David: The flight from UK are off because of all the media attention and they can't get insurance. We can still go ahead with the second part, extract on Saturday to Tashkent and back to UK. I've just had Peter Egan on the phone as he has been contacted by some military guys saying that we have got to go dark as Pen and the team are now sitting duck in Kabul and ISIS is on the ground and we should say nothing until they land back in the UK.

[26/08/2021, 11:19:20] Ian: if he can be. where and which group

[26/08/2021, 11:19:48] Nina: Whoops!! I forgot the main man. Sorry - I'll get him on now

[26/08/2021, 11:20:05] Nina: You added Pen Farthing

Finally I was added – thanks Nina.

[26/08/2021, 11:20:48] Ian: flights are all stopped cos US nabbed them all. not because of us

[26/08/2021, 11:21:05] Ian: when is the call?

[26/08/2021, 11:23:23] Sam: So we need to know where that information came from. Facts. Cold facts.

[26/08/2021, 11:24:26] Ian: yes I suggest a group call in 5?

[26/08/2021, 11:25:03] Nina: No way to do group WhatsApp calls with Pen sorry - roaming just doesn't have that capability over there. He's picking up things fairly regularly though so…

[26/08/2021, 11:25:03] Kaisa: We need this confirmed, and if so no further media show.

[26/08/2021, 11:28:39] David: It's confirmed the UK flight is off but the two flights out of Kabul on the Friday back will still happen

This part of the plan I still struggle with and it was news to me… two flights to collect me, staff, and animals. I had no idea how that would work in practice.

[26/08/2021, 12:21:48] Dan: Nina, are you coming back on the Zoom call?

[26/08/2021, 12:23:27] Nina: Is it open again? Sure

[26/08/2021, 12:25:06] Dan: The more the merrier!

[26/08/2021, 12:44:36] Ann: Great line from an article in the Independent; "We praise dogs as "heroes" when we push them into wars but then say "they're just dogs" when someone wants to save them from war-torn Afghanistan"

[26/08/2021, 13:12:24] Ian: Nina just sent copy please proof approve, tweak, whatever

[26/08/2021, 13:29:00] Dominic: I have spoken to Stephanie has some good security contacts on ground who might be able to help Pen I will link them up now

[26/08/2021, 13:29:27] Nina: Brilliant. No stone left unturned with this I think…

[26/08/2021, 13:35:40] Kaisa: [thumbs up emoji]

[26/08/2021, 13:38:10] Sam: IF ANYONE IS TALKING TO PEN, I NEED HIM TO READ MY LATEST MESSAGE NOW PLEASE

[26/08/2021, 13:50:27] Ian: not in comms

[26/08/2021, 13:51:17] Ian: how else can we get him message. Vet staff have phones. anyone know

[26/08/2021, 13:51:49] Sam: Don't call him now. He's got the message

[26/08/2021, 14:05:06] Dan: Update from cargo company: "UPDATE: Tashkent handling confirmed, animals will have assistance in cargo terminal, probably some of the supervisors may enter the facility as well. Entire group will have hot meal provided in the transit area. ALL FLIGHTS ARE NOW CONFIRMED" [26/08/2021, 14:12:04] Nina: Roger that Dan!! Thanks - Pen only in the #SitRep group now. So go for it on this in terms of chatter, anyone on SitRep group Pen will be on there but I will also try and get anything really urgent in front of him. If you let me know. No promises though as getting increasingly hard to reach him

[26/08/2021, 14:13:59] Dan: A further message from the air charter to Pen: "@Pen Farthing did the bring your trucks to the front of the queue? OK, I have report you have passed Talib gate, correct?"

[26/08/2021, 14:18:07] Nina: HELP!!!!

[26/08/2021, 14:19:06] Nina: audio omitted

(My voice note telling Nina that we had been stopped by the Taliban from entering)

[26/08/2021, 14:19:52] Nina: We have 5 mins to sort - listen above

[26/08/2021, 14:20:24] Nina: Who can we get to help? We need the highest level American any of us know

[26/08/2021, 14:20:51] Nina: Dan? Spencer? Dominic? We need a very top American person to allow these 68 through

[26/08/2021, 14:21:20] Dora the Explorer: I will contact Trudy in case she can help

[26/08/2021, 14:21:46] Dan: I am calling.

[26/08/2021, 14:22:45] Ian: fantastic

[26/08/2021, 14:23:11] Sam: Someone give me Dan's number now please thanks

[26/08/2021, 14:23:50] Ann: I have forwarded the number to you

[26/08/2021, 14:24:19] Dora the Explorer: Left message for Trudy, will try again.

[26/08/2021, 14:24:43] Kaisa: It's UK!!!!!!

[26/08/2021, 14:25:36] Nina: They are UK approved but it is America that the Taliban are using as an excuse.

[26/08/2021, 14:26:09] Dan: Whoever has the best facts, please call me now

[26/08/2021, 14:26:15] Kaisa: It's just an excuse! Bribe, insist on talking to highest commander of Taliban

[26/08/2021, 14:27:00] David: The guy who we have charted the plane from has guys on the ground there and in coms with the TB

[26/08/2021, 14:27:39] Nina: Dan is calling. Dominic calling Spencer

[26/08/2021, 14:27:50] Nina: Trudy can you please please call Boris?

[26/08/2021, 14:27:54] Sam: LEFT messages FOR DAN

[26/08/2021, 14:28:00] Nina: They are 300 yards from British held territory

[26/08/2021, 14:28:23] Nina: I can confirm TB will allow Pen and the animals through but NOT the 68

[26/08/2021, 14:28:30] Nina: 300 yards to go.

[26/08/2021, 14:28:54] David: tell Pen he has got to ring this no +998*******45

[26/08/2021, 14:28:56] Nina: Dan/Dominic/Trudy - this has to come from way up high in the US power machine now

[26/08/2021, 14:29:02] Kaisa: I'm calling the most senior people I know

[26/08/2021, 14:29:06] Nina: Who is that number David??

[26/08/2021, 14:29:38] David: The guys on the ground from the charter company who are working with the TB

[26/08/2021, 14:29:54] Nina: He is keeping them sweet for now but this has to happen immediately

[26/08/2021, 14:30:23] David: If he rings them immediately this will work as there is a trade-off to be done

[26/08/2021, 14:32:29] Nina: Right told him that David. Thanks

[26/08/2021, 14:32:35] Dan: I am framing up the problem for a US Senator to jump on it. But I'm guessing this will get more attention from the British govt side of the house.

[26/08/2021, 14:33:03] Dora the Explorer: Still not heard from Trudy….

[26/08/2021, 14:33:07] Nina: Calling equivalent in US??

[26/08/2021, 14:33:41] Kaisa: Do whatever, I just called Larry ffs. It's clearly Taliban keeping an order from US troops, while this convoy is UK issue ! Wrong orders. Misunderstanding

[26/08/2021, 14:34:17] Nina: Someone pls keep trying Trudy to get to Boris

[26/08/2021, 14:34:43] Dora the Explorer: Spoke to Trudy, she is ringing around on our behalf.

[26/08/2021, 14:35:01] Nina: Thank you. I'll keep trying Raab's Secretary

[26/08/2021, 14:35:53] Kaisa: I'm assuming this is direct orders on the ground from US highest commander to Taliban on the ground. Can highest commander of anything on ground walk over and give a thumbs up to Taliban that these are going to UK, not US

[26/08/2021, 14:39:21] Nina: Anyone find out anything about this US policy that came in like 3 hours ago??? No more Afghans into airport without US visas??

[26/08/2021, 14:40:30] Kaisa: But they're going to UK !! [three facepalm emojis]

I had no idea that the US had changed its policy just three hours ago. As you can see, neither did the evac team nor, presumably, the British government.

Standing just a yard or so from the Taliban commander, I stared directly at him as I lowered myself into a kneeling position on the road. My left knee rested on the dotted white line which divided the two halves of the main thoroughfare towards the international and domestic terminals. On one side was the Taliban. On the other were international flights out of Afghanistan. I needed to get the lorries and buses across that line to safety.

I pressed my hands together as if praying and did something I had never ever done to any human being before: I begged for the safe passage of our convoy like a man about to be executed. I appealed to what I hoped was humanity buried deep within him.

It was futile exercise. His face remained unemotional. His eyes were looking directly at me but he was not seeing me.

There were no other sounds. His security team of the three Talibs just stood to one side, silently watching my every move. Their assault rifles were held in a semi-ready position, draped against the soft leather magazine pouches worn around their chests. None had applied the safety catch on their weapons. Worse still, one fingered the trigger on his weapon far too much. We were mere feet away from two buses full of women and children. A stray bullet from any one of these rifles would tear through the outer skin of the bus without slowing down. The thought was unimaginable.

"Please. Just let us go down this road to the British checkpoint. Let the British deal with us. It is all good." I realised my voice sounded defeated but I tried my best to reassure him. I eyed his every facial expression in those brief moments. I willed the Talib commander into letting us pass. I knew if we could make it to a friendly British face then this ordeal was over. But that opportunity seemed to be rapidly slipping away.

"No," was his simple reply as he waved his hand dismissively. I could feel the utter lack of compassion in the way he said it. "No."

Earlier that day he had apparently been given an order by the Americans to let no Afghan into the airport without a valid visa. An ARAP issued by the British government was not enough.

"Pleeease," I gasped as I implored him to allow us to travel just another 300 yards further into the airport. I could see the next airport circle just 100 yards ahead.

I just had to get this convoy beyond that and all this would be over. I had never felt so desperate in my life.

I glanced across to see the faces of young children pressed up against the smudged windows of the two buses, unaware of the seriousness of the drama currently playing out, eagerly anticipating new lives that awaited them just those few hundred yards away. And then I saw the look on some of their parents' faces, mothers and fathers wracked with the stress from the last few days and now terrified for what could happen next.

The commander's face turned a burgundy shade at my continued attempts to sway the decision he had already made. To allow me to pass now would be to lose face in front of his men. And a Talib commander was not about to capitulate to the pleading nagging of a foreigner.

He dismissed me once more with a brief wave of his hand, turned and yelled in Dari. I immediately understood what he was shouting as the steel muzzle of an AK-47 pressed into the side of my temple.

"I have told you!" the commander shrieked in English. "You can go and take your animals with you but the Afghans stay."

The striking feature about the commander was his strong English accent.

The silence after the commander's outburst became deafening. Time stood still.

I calculated the half-second it would take for me to grab the muzzle of the AK-47 pressing against my temple with my left hand in a simple forward gesturing motion. My hands held aloft in surrender, were already raised in the air which saved valuable time. If I pushed the muzzle away in a sweeping motion, preventing my brains from being splattered all over the black tarmacked road, I could then jerk the weapon violently backwards, which would ensure the guard impulsively reacted by involuntary squeezing the trigger. The weapons muzzle would now spew 7.62 calibre bullets in the direction of the two currently shocked guards and of course, the commander. They would die at the hands of their own comrade.

As all of this was happening I would be driving upwards to a fighting stance and thrusting my right hand into his Adam's apple, instantly rendering him out of the game. I figured if we were quick, then Farid and I could gather the fallen guards' weapons and hold off the Taliban gathered back down at the main gate, whilst the convoy gunned it for the British lines.

In those milliseconds I'd thought the entire scenario through.

But I had no idea if there really was a British presence 300 yards further up the airport road. And if there was, would they come out in support? I no longer had a deep confidence that they would. So we could be in the firefight of our lives and yet have no backup to save the day and rain hell upon the advancing Taliban.

Sensibility prevailed. There were two packed buses, mostly full of women and children, just yards to my right. I had made them my responsibility.

And as Mujtaba had rightly pointed out during our mad

dash around Kabul's congested streets to capture the mange-covered dog earlier in the summer: *"We are not in a movie, Sir!"*

I was no action hero. So I continued with the only other option available when outnumbered and with a gun to your head.

"Please reconsider," I pleaded, looking directly at the commander's uncompassionate eyes.

The muzzle pressed harder. There was no life flashing through my head as I anticipated the click of the trigger being pulled and my head exploding all over the oil-stained surface of the road.

I simply registered I had lost. We had achieved so much in getting this far but it was for nothing. I felt a hand on my right shoulder pulling me backward slowly.

"Mr Pen," a shaken voice said, "we must go. Now!"

I turned my head to register Farid's arm pulling at me. I nodded in his direction as I steadied myself to a standing position.

"Ok, ok," I stated in the direction of the Taliban commander, "we will leave."

I guess my face held the resigned look of a broken man. But inside I just wanted to break his neck. The particular level of hatred reserved for a fellow human had replaced the sense of helplessness that had overwhelmed me moments earlier.

Then we all felt the vibration. It rolled along the ground and travelled up through our bodies from our feet. The delayed *boom* rolled across us seconds later.

There was no question as to what it was. As one with the Taliban, we all turned and faced the direction of the Abbey

Gate about half a mile away, hidden from view by administration buildings and jet-fuel storage tanks.

I looked at Farid, eyes wide.

The Taliban's walkie-talkies suddenly burst in to life, unintelligible shouting streaming across the airways.

Farid was listening intently to the commander yell into his phone and he then confirmed what I had already guessed.

"Suicide attack."

"Where?" I asked, although it was obvious.

"Abbey Gate."

The commander ended his heated call and simply shouted "GO!" as he turned on his heel and strode off in the direction of an approaching vehicle.

His security detail closed around myself and Farid, prodding us back toward the lead truck. I quickly pushed them away and ran towards the second truck where a tense Aman was waiting.

In Dari I simply said, "Dafta," (Office) whilst shaking my head. He reluctantly understood.

I sprinted to the first bus. Hamida was waiting for me by the door. I shook my head. "We need to go back to the office. They won't let us in."

Her face remained expressionless as she absorbed what I had just said and ultimately what it meant. She would not be leaving Afghanistan. We had been turned away by the Taliban obeying orders from Joe Biden and we weren't even going to America. I wanted to hug her and say it would be okay. But hugging would have not gone down well with the panicking Taliban who had been left to remove us from the airport. Besides, what assurance could I give her? It fucking wasn't going to be okay.

I ran on to tell Zahra, who was captain of the second family bus.

I was distracted by the shouting from behind me. The Taliban security detail were becoming agitated at the lack of movement by the vehicles. Turning all four vehicles in the tight confines of the terminal approach road took longer than I wanted to. All the time the Taliban fighters were now aggressively pointing their rifles at us.

"Let's go Farid Jan," I encouraged in my best urgent-without-out-trying-to-sound-urgent voice. I watched in the truck's side mirror as the remaining bus finished the three-point turn so we could drive out the way we'd just come.

There was no time for disappointment. We were being thrown back out in the unsecured areas of the airport approach. And potentially right into the potential blast zone of another suicide bomber. Either of our buses crammed with the women and young children would be an ideal target for a suicide bomber seeking a high casualty rate.

"Let's go!" I yelled as Farid slammed the truck into first and our old chariot trundled forward with a jerk.

I took one last look in the side mirror. Receding slowly in the far distance, I could just about make out the end of the long drive way that I knew disappeared into the trees before revealing the large open expanse of the domestic and then international terminal buildings.

Somewhere back there would have been the British military checkpoint and home.

Some might say getting back to my Kaisa's side should have been my priority, that I could have been driving down that road to the welcome sight of the maroon-bereted lads and lasses of 16 Air Assault.

But in that split second whilst kneeling in the middle of the airport approach road with a loaded gun pointed to my head, I had made my mind up.

[26/08/2021, 14:48:18] Nina: Pen and ppl ok.

[26/08/2021, 14:48:27] Nina: can start to hear gun fire

[26/08/2021, 14:48:27] Dora the Explorer: [prayer emoji]

[26/08/2021, 14:48:37] Tom: [thumbs up emoji]

[26/08/2021, 14:48:52] Nina: Told him to use the threat of VBIED to let the TB stay where they are for now

[26/08/2021, 14:49:05] Nina: He's trying to charm them but they're getting angry

[26/08/2021, 14:49:41] Nina: And want to turf them out. If they get pushed back beyond boundary of wall again, they'll never step back over again

[26/08/2021, 14:50:08] Nina: Sarah says FCDO won't intervene. Try MoD she suggests.

[26/08/2021, 14:50:33] Dominic: Pass the buck time

[26/08/2021, 14:50:36] Nina: Who can call Peter Quentin? Leo Dochety?? Wallace??

Peter Quentin was the special advisor the Defence Secretary Ben Wallace. Leo Docherty was Parliamentary Under Secretary of State at the Foreign, Commonwealth and Development Office.

[26/08/2021, 14:50:49] Nina: Trudy!!!!! We need you. Please call Dochety

[26/08/2021, 14:50:53] Kaisa: Commander on ground, no time for high up people

[26/08/2021, 14:51:33] Nina: TB commander on ground.

[26/08/2021, 14:51:42] Sam: Pen says he needs help from Americans within next 5 mins or they are all back out on the road

[26/08/2021, 14:51:47] Ian: I will call Pete Quentin

[26/08/2021, 14:52:07] Dora the Explorer: Sam, I know everyone is trying to seek approval upwards, but any chance you could see if 16 Air Assault can help? Tiny chance?

[26/08/2021, 14:53:27] Dan: We need friendlies inside the wire to intervene.

[26/08/2021, 14:53:58] Kaisa: Forget approval, or… work on that!!! [thumbs up emoji] but they need a solider walking over and confirming that they have UK visas and give thumbs up

[26/08/2021, 14:54:37] Nina: American and/or Brit soldier??

[26/08/2021, 14:55:15] Nina: They're throwing them out

[26/08/2021, 14:55:21] Kaisa: Anyone that can go over and say yes

[26/08/2021, 14:55:39] Nina: Anything they can delay with?

[26/08/2021, 14:55:42] Ian: can we put this on media????

[26/08/2021, 14:55:51] Nina: Trudy - please call Dochety.

[26/08/2021, 14:56:01] Ian: BBC will put it out

[26/08/2021, 14:56:23] Ian: answer, or I will

[26/08/2021, 14:56:34] Sam: Have contacted link
into Ops to ask for someone to go over. Don't rely
on this. Keep trying

[26/08/2021, 14:57:10] Tom: Bugger

[26/08/2021, 14:57:24] Nina: Dominic - didn't
Spencer have links to Colin Powell??? Can't believe
I'm saying this

[26/08/2021, 14:57:24] Tom: Trying vets and SF
contact

[26/08/2021, 14:58:25] Ian: look shall I out this
on BBC get defence sec called in US

[26/08/2021, 14:58:36] Nina: Yes

[26/08/2021, 14:59:10] Nina: Someone tweet TB
spokesman from earlier

[26/08/2021, 14:59:17] Trudy MP: Pen just rang,
he's going to try to head back to compound was
forced out at gun point

[26/08/2021, 15:15:34] Nina: Second explosion.
They need to get out of the immediate area.

[26/08/2021, 15:15:41] Sam: Thanks!

[26/08/2021, 15:15:43] Nina: From Raab's office
again

[26/08/2021, 15:17:24] Dan: If there were ever a
good time to convene a Zoom call, this might be it.

[26/08/2021, 15:19:35] Tom: SBS contact sadly out:
Hi Tom, probably not I'm afraid. Partly that I'm
on holiday and not involved directly with evac, and
secondly that I've used my chips trying to help get
a few people out for people already to the extent
of annoying the team who are running things. I've
just read Ben Wallace's statement on Nowzad saying
will help but not give greater priority than to

others etc- and I don't feel me piping up will help
things I'm afraid"

SBS is Special Boat Service – Special Forces basically.

[26/08/2021, 15:19:48] Nina: See zoom link above
from me

[26/08/2021, 15:20:57] Kaisa: Abbey gate.
Single explosion. Both Afghan and International
Casualties. No numbers yet.

[26/08/2021, 15:21:20] Nina: Zoom info please get on

[26/08/2021, 15:21:33] Kaisa: Pen is heading back

[26/08/2021, 15:21:41] Nina: [thumbs up emoji]

[26/08/2021, 15:22:10] Dan: Back where? Airport or
Clinic?

[26/08/2021, 15:23:24] Sam: Can't get on zoom

[26/08/2021, 15:23:38] Kaisa: Dunno. I said move to
safe location close by as we're calling everyone,
he said the area is turning into chaos and I heard
shooting pretty close, then he said 2 minutes to
someone in Dari, then he said we're leaving, then
connection lost.

Hundreds of people in front of us were running for safety in
all directions. They were fleeing the Abbey Gate and the suicide bombing there. We were fleeing the south gate and the
hysterical Talib commander there. We were converging on
the same space. The Taliban, in response to the widespread
panic and mounting chaos, fired tear gas into this crowd. Into
us.

There were screams of shock and pain. Yells for loved
ones as they stumbled, running or hobbling away. Some were
holding blood-soaked clothing as they fled from where they
had just been.

The acrid smell of smoke was overpowering. My eyes were still streaming from the tear gas but my vision was more or less at an acceptable level to operate. I couldn't see through the smoke that wafted across the airport circle. I dropped out of the cab and turned to run back to check on the other vehicles and their passengers.

When the tear gas bomb had exploded, I'd held my breath and squinted my eyes shut. Basic military training.

Farid did not have that training. He inhaled and kept his eyes open. As soon as he started spluttering and crying, I yelled at him to bring the truck to a slow stop. He was about to be fully incapacitated.

If we had kept driving forward we would, without a doubt, have run over some of those fleeing.

The rapidly fading sunlight was not helping matters. Everything was dusty grey. The noise was terrifying. Automatic gunfire rang out all around us. Occasional flashbang bombs would add to the confusion. The stink of tear gas was everywhere.

Marine Sergeant mode kicked in. I needed to evacuate our team out of Dodge ASAP.

I left Farid lying on his side gagging from inhaling the tear gas. Mujtaba wasn't fairing much better. The other three vehicles had all come to a stop behind our lead truck. Occupants of the first bus were in various stages of gagging and crying and that included all of the children we had with us. It was carnage. As I looked through the glass windows of the bus all I saw were terrified faces staring back out at me.

"Tell them not to rub their eyes," I half-yelled, half-coughed to Hamida. My face was burning. Being tear-gassed sucked.

I looked back at Aman who was driving the second truck.

Anywhere else it would have been comical, but I stood doing a charades skit of turning a steering wheel to him. In between fits of coughing he nodded and gave a thumbs up. The further I ran back, the less the families were feeling the effects of the tear gas. We must have taken a direct hit on the lead truck.

I waved at one of the young children on the second bus, our last vehicle, his eyes wide and pressed up against the bus window, staring out at the disturbing scenes unfolding across the airport circle.

I slammed my hands to cover my ears as just behind me a Talib unloaded a full magazine on automatic into the air in a bizarre attempt to hurry the injured up in leaving the scene of the suicide bombing.

"Fuck," I mouthed, it was loud. I turned to berate him. I was beyond caring, but he was already moving off toward a family struggling to carry a body, whether they were dead or injured I don't know. The lights were out across this part of the city. I had no idea if it was a result of the suicide bombing.

With the drivers of the last three vehicles seemingly capable of driving, albeit slowly, I ran back to our lead truck and jumped into the driver's seat, pushing Farid out of the way. Both him and Mujtaba were still suffering the tear gas effects.

I crunched the gear into first again and punched the accelerator. We lurched forward. I checked the rear-view mirrors to ensure all our vehicles were moving.

Slowly and carefully, we made our way back to the Nowzad compound. I desperately wanted to check on the dogs and cats. They would have been tear-gassed too and experienced the shock and trauma of the automatic weapons being fired irresponsibly in the air. Those bullets would have had to come down somewhere. But I couldn't do anything about it until we were safely back in the compound.

–

I never actually got to see any of the messages in the newly formed WhatsApp group until I did the research for this book. I cannot even begin to comprehend the frustration and feelings of helplessness that my friends felt whilst trying to work out the problems that seemed to continually stack up against our operation. While Nowzad is about rescuing animals, the team we had around us was also deeply concerned and committed to the families and staff. They were then and still are the best.

They never ever gave up. They worked throughout every night of the evacuation without question or complaint. Nina was given an ultimatum during her training to be a paramedic: stop supporting this rescue and attend every class or you will be dismissed.

Without hesitation she left the training knowing full well she would not be reaccepted. Her priority became ensuring Operation Ark was a success. Sam stopped her house renovation that was on a tight financial deadline to use every contact she had to bring about the success of Operation Ark. Dora the Explorer left a family holiday to ensure she could be in on the meetings and support our evacuation. Jen found herself strapped to her laptop and calling Mujtaba in Kabul day and night as she filed license after license with the Department for Environment and Rural Affairs. She was attempting to pull off the single ever biggest import of dogs and cats to the United Kingdom on a single flight and it consumed her every waking minute.

Ian found himself sidelined by fellow veterinarians and his professional association for his support of our operation, which was being accused of putting "pets over people" even whilst I was driving our convoy of men, women, and children through tear gas. But Ian never backed down.

Dan operated with a twelve-and-half-hour time difference ensuring he was present for every call. David tirelessly investigated every possible option from the many thousands of contacts we were receiving daily with advice on how to make Operation Ark a success. Ann, David's wife, was bombarded with support and queries every time we posted on social media. She endeavoured to answer everyone as best she could. At one point our server held over 39,000 emails collected in a three-day period from Nowzad supporters.

The team never ever contemplated giving up and for me that means I will never ever be able to thank them enough for what they did during those two weeks of utter desperation.

Whilst I was kneeling on the tarmac road, the evac team did what they could in the heat of the moment, scrambling to ask everyone they thought might have connections to make a difference.

Yet, not a single person with any power to intervene answered our calls.

And this is when the incompetence and disregard feels personal. It tips into feeling like malice. Or perhaps I should put it this way: incompetence and disregard is inherently malicious when people's lives are in danger. I truly wonder if they had counted on us just giving up and the whole sorry saga being forgotten in the greater horror of the overall evacuation chaos.

On that fateful night of the 26th of August 2021, an Islamic

State suicide bomber detonated his ball bearing-packed explosive vest in the canal route between the Baron Hotel and the Abbey Gate, killing thirteen members of the United States military.

Sgt. Johanny Rosario Pichardo
Sgt. Nicole L. Gee
Staff Sgt. Darin T. Hoover
Cpl. Hunter Lopez
Cpl. Daegan W. Page
Cpl. Humberto A. Sanchez
Lance Cpl. David L. Espinoza
Lance Cpl. Jared M. Schmitz
Lance Cpl. Rylee J. McCollum
Lance Cpl. Dylan R. Merola
Lance Cpl. Kareem M. Nikoui
Navy Corpsman Maxton W. Soviak
Staff Sgt. Ryan C. Knauss

Exact numbers vary according to which source you use, but it is confirmed that over 170 civilians, all Afghans attempting to flee Afghanistan for a better life in the West, were also killed in the bombing. Having served as a Royal Marine on active duty and witnessed man at his worst, I can honestly say that the number of lives lost that night is beyond comprehension.

I had always said that the Abbey Gate was too much of a choke point. Being brutally honest, I was surprised it had taken as long as it did before an IS-K militant detonated himself amongst the thousands trying to flee.

It was the sole reason I had never even contemplated taking the convoy into the Abbey Gate entrance. I knew the area well and I truly believed it was a death trap waiting to happen. Regrettably those fears were realised.

The decision I took, to use Kabul Airport's main entrance, even though the British had told me to head toward the Abbey Gate, saved our lives that day.

It is a humbling thought.

27 August 2021

Still recovering from the tear gas attack, we had travelled less than a kilometre from the bedlam of the airport roundabout, when we encountered yet another group of Taliban at a checkpoint who had no intention of letting us pass.

After realising we were transporting dogs, the commander of this checkpoint produced a phone with an image of a blindfolded and plastic-cuffed inmate from Guantánamo Bay, kneeling on the floor clad in the infamous orange jumpsuit. A snarling German Shepard was straining at the end of its leash right by the side of the detainee's head.

The Talib was visibly angry.

"These dogs?" he shouted pointing to the image. "You have these dogs?"

I shook my head. "No. Sag serac," I said as calmly as I could. "Street dogs."

But this Talib was having none of it. He kept yelling at me. I'd had a hell of a day. The gun to the head. The disappointment. The frustration. The suicide bomber. The shooting and the tear gas. The chaos. We all just wanted to go home. And now this.

It all became too much.

I lost my rag with him. I yelled directly into his face that I just wanted to go back to the clinic, to go home.

This, clearly, was not a great idea. It was absolutely one of the stupidest arguments I have ever had with a guy holding a gun. The Taliban were a law unto themselves. He could have just fired his rifle at the two trucks on automatic. Nobody apart from me would have intervened. And who knows what would have happened then.

Farid stopped the situation from escalating by dragging me to one side to calm me down. I needed the time-out to stop myself from doing something we would all regret.

Finally, once he was satisfied we weren't carrying dogs from Guantánamo, our convoy was allowed to continue on our way.

We arrived back at the Nowzad compound after that. For Farid though, the chaos didn't end there. After leaving Nowzad around eleven o'clock that night in a yellow taxi with his wife and three daughters for the short journey back to their home, he paid the taxi driver and bundled his family through the front door, everyone beyond tired and stressed but extremely happy to be home.

Except Farid never had all his family. His eldest child had climbed over the back seat into the open boot of the taxi estate car without anyone noticing to catch some sleep. As taxis do not belong to a firm as such, it took Farid nearly four hours to find his daughter, still curled up in the boot compartment. The taxi driver had made several pick-ups, completely unaware of her presence.

Meanwhile, I had my own crisis.

–

As soon as we arrived at back at the compound, Mujtaba and Hamida cornered me. "You must leave, Sir," Hamida urged, staring straight at me. Her face was composed, but I could see the sadness in her eyes.

"No, I will stay and cross into Pakistan with you," I replied. How that would work I had no idea.

"No, Sir," Mujtaba jumped in. "We will stand out too much with you and the dogs and cats." He meant that my presence with the animals would endanger them all, the staff, their families, the children, exponentially more, and thereby ensure that none of us would get out.

"Take the animals on the flight," he continued. "We will be safer on the journey without you."

Hamida nodded her agreement as he spoke. I looked at them both. They were deadly seriously. The decision had been made for me. I also knew they were right. The clock was ticking. The Taliban were unpredictable. The British government, whether out of sheer incompetence or otherwise, had delayed and delayed giving Nowzad's entitled Afghans their paperwork until it was too late and the Americans had shut down access. We had not seen that one coming. My solid plan to fly us all out with the staff in the passenger seats and the animals in the cargo hold was not going to work. We needed a Plan B.

Two days before, on the 25th of August 10.40pm (UK Local), Ben Wallace was quoted in a Guardian article by Dan Sabbagh and Aubrey Allegretti: "I recommend that they [the evacuees] try and make it to the border." That was the only other option.

I reluctantly nodded. I had no choice.

I would escape Afghanistan with the dog and cats alone, whilst the team faced the prospect of travelling overland to slip into Pakistan.

I hugged Mujtaba. "Ok, Lala, I will see you in England my friend." I turned and hugged Hamida too. It was against the rules, but I no longer cared, I needed the hug. She hugged me back. "Thank you. I will see you in England soon," I said.

Her lovely smile came back briefly. "Yes, inshallah."

It was around eleven o'clock at night by the time the team

had finished unloading the dogs and cats from their crates and returned the trucks to the secret parking spot. I ensured I spoke to everyone who had remained at the house overnight, wishing them well for the overland journey to Pakistan and promising them I would see them in England soon. I tried to remain positive and upbeat in front of everyone. But I was drained and heartbroken.

As the 26th ended and the 27th started, I convened a Zoom call with the evac team to let them know that it was just me and the dogs and cats now attempting to enter the airport.

Once the meeting ended, I carried out a final once-around the compound. The dogs and cats that I could see in the darkness were devouring the recently provided food and enjoying the ability to stretch their legs. Basir was busy washing out the full complement of travel crates.

The evac committee worked through the night and by the morning had already split into two teams. Nina and David, heading up the continued work of securing the permissions for the chartered flight I would be taking. Sam and Dora the Explorer concentrated on figuring out how to transport the staff to the border area and gain the necessary permissions for them to officially – and therefore safely – cross the Torkham border into Pakistan.

We decided to leave at nine o'clock in the morning on the dot. The staff swiftly loaded the dogs and cats back onto the trucks, still sticking rigidly to the load plan. I guessed the dogs wondered what the hell was going on. If only they knew what was to come. I looked on totally terrified of how I was going to unload the trucks on my own and then load the aircraft according to the carefully configured cargo hold loading plan, again potentially on my own.

"One problem at a time, Farthing," I reminded myself. No point stressing unnecessarily. Probably best concentrating on how I got back into the bloody airport for a second time.

The Friday morning drive back to the airport was quiet, a world apart from the Taliban-led convoy of the first attempt. Neither Farid nor I spoke. Behind us, Amanullah followed in the second lorry. There were no cars on the roads and the streets were mostly empty. It felt like a city resigned to its fate.

The entry to the south gate had been straightforward. The Talib security recognised us from the day before and allowed us passage straight into the airport approach road. They had extended the cordon to include most of the forty-metre road now. As it should have been from day one of the evacuation.

For nearly fifteen minutes I watched the same Talib commander as yesterday, the one who'd put a gun to my head and deny us safe passage, just stand on this side of the barrier and talk into his phone. We still needed his permission to cross over the line to the international side. He appeared completely oblivious to the presence of two lorries stacked high with dogs and cats, which really was not an everyday occurrence in Kabul. I suppose he had seen them yesterday.

"What a dickhead," I thought. I wanted to punch him. And what were his guards going to do? Shoot me? The British *fucking* parachute regiment were standing just feet away, across a piece of barbed wire, and they ate barbed wire for breakfast, or so they liked to tell us Royal Marines.

I was distracted from thoughts of violence as I observed a family of four walk towards the coiled razor wire that marked out the safety of Britain from where I was stood, which was

Taliban central. The father was dressed smartly in his grey suit with a striking red tie. His wife followed in her black headscarf, carrying a small black leather handbag.

Two young girls maybe no older than ten or twelve, walked in line behind their mother and father. The oldest girl wore a white pattern dress, with flowery shoulder pads that reminded me of tea coasters my gran used to have on her small living room table. On her back she carried a huge red rucksack, oversized for her small frame. Under the dress that covered down to her knees she wore faded blue jeans. She covered her head as required by a tan headscarf.

The family walked forward towards their freedom, past where I was stood with my two trucks, Farid slumped with his eyes closed in the first vehicle and Aman watching in from the cab of the second one. I stood there in the stifling heat and felt an impending sense of unease.

The commander directed them to stand alongside the makeshift barbed wire barrier, the Brits on the other side, and called for their passports to be handed over.

I watched as the father searched in his bag for their collective passports and held them for the commander to collect for inspection. The husband looked reassuringly at his wife and then his daughters.

The commander produced a sheet of paper from the pocket of his long grey trousers. I watched intently as he compared the passports to whatever detail the paper held.

Suddenly he erupted, waving his arms and shaking his head violently as he yelled at his guards whilst pointing at the now terrified-looking father, who immediately realised he had been found out. One guard rushed headlong into restraining the father who was by now pleading rapidly at the commander in Dari that was far too fast for me to translate. The imploring look in his eyes was heartbreaking.

The guard on the orders of the overstimulated commander dragged the smaller-framed father away by his arm, away from his family. His wife dropped to her knees and attempted to grab her husband's leg to prevent him from being taken.

She missed, instead falling to the ground screaming, her headscarf dislodged, black hair spilling out around her anguished face. His young children begin to rush to their father's side, but the second guard prevented them by crouching forward with outstretched arms and yelling incoherently at them.

I braced up. Fully alert to intervene. I went to take a step forward.

"Mr Pen, NO!" shouted Farid from the cab of the truck. I had no idea he had been awake.

My outstretched foot swung back so I was standing upright, arms by my side ready to charge forward. I clocked the two British soldiers standing just twenty-five feet or so away on the other side of the barbed wire barricade. They were watching. Observing in silence. They hadn't raised their weapons in preparation to intervene.

The closest soldier spotted me. With a resounding shake of his head, he mouthed, "No."

My heart was racing.

"Is nobody going to intervene?" I shouted as just five feet from where I stood, the husband was dragged screaming from his tearful wife and daughters back into the bowels of Kabul. As he was led away, the poor man kept attempting to turn to look at his family. His red tie draped over his shoulder as he was jerked forward by his overbearing guard.

To make it this far along the airport drive had required the family of four to have the correct paperwork. They had clearly been called forward by the British. I don't know what was on that piece of paper. I suspect that he was on some list the Taliban had drawn up of most wanted. I'm guessing that meant he'd worked in a senior position for the previous government or the security services. Now that father would never make his promised flight out. Ever.

People have gone out of their way to blame me for rescuing dogs and cats over people. First and foremost, that isn't true. But secondly, what the fuck else could I have done? I was powerless. I wasn't Rambo, I couldn't just grab the man from the Taliban and take him with me. All I could do was watch as someone's husband, a father, was just taken – and no one intervened.

British soldiers, the only ones who could have prevented it, stood by and watched, unable to cross over a piece of barbed wire to intervene. As I know only too well, orders are orders and their rules of engagement, which vary for each conflict zone they serve in, denied them the ability to intervene. Suits, thousands of miles away and safely shielded from the raw inhumanity as it unfolded, dictated the rules of engagement.

That day they were operating under orders that only allowed them to act in self-defence if they were being attacked by an effective enemy.

The dynamics were clear. On this side of the barbed wire where I languished with the lorries, the Taliban were completely in charge. If they chose to not let me cross that line, then there was absolutely nothing the Brits were going to do or could do to stop them.

The anger I feel about what I witnessed that day lingers and forever will. I have never told anyone that story until now. Not even Kaisa. But maybe I should have, so that she would have understood my sadness and anger.

So let me make this 100% clear to those who believed wholeheartedly in the blatant lies – I never ever put British soldiers in harm's way. I couldn't have. Because they had orders not to risk themselves for anyone, much less for a bunch of cats and dogs. Find one member of 16 Air Assault who will testify he or she stepped over that barbed wire against orders and "escorted" me in.

Once the husband had been dragged a sufficient distant back down the airport terminal drive, the distraught mother and her two daughters were ushered to the barbed wire divide. On the request of the Taliban commander the barrier was removed to one side and the family was released into the hands of the British military manning their side of checkpoint. With no choice but to continue with their mother, the two young girls shuffled forward, crying and constantly turning to look for their father who was by now out of view. The barrier was replaced and an identical routine with the passports was carried out by the British paratroopers.

I looked around bewildered, trying to justify what I had just witnessed. I stared up at Farid and immediately saw his fear. The Taliban could so easily do that to whomever they wished, and nobody was going to prevent it. You would just disappear.

I eased myself to the ground. My backside met the tarmacked road with a thump. I leant back against the driver's side tyre. The tread was almost worn to nothing in places. Still, this was probably its last journey so I didn't care about tread depth of tyres. I stretched my legs out, noted my boots truly needed a polish and closed my eyes. I tried to switch off from what I had just seen, ready for whatever was coming my way next by taking long deep breaths through my nose and blowing out through my mouth.

"You need to get out of here, lad," I thought to myself as the sun felt fiercely hot on my closed eyelids, "This place is going to rat shit fast."

–

When that smug bastard finally decided I was allowed to cross, it was a straightforward procedure. The Taliban commander signalled to the British soldiers, who in turn slid the barbed wire to one side and we drove across the line into the British held side of the airport at around 1800hrs (Kabul local time) on the 27th of August.

Farid and Amanullah dropped down out of the cabs, we hugged and shook hands, and they took off running back down the way we had driven several hours before along the airport approach road. The threat of another suicide attack was on everyone's minds. We had agreed they were not to take any chances but keep running until they were well outside the cordon. They would hail a taxi to take them back to the Nowzad compound.

An army major strode up to me as I stood outside the lead truck. We weren't going anywhere until somebody offered to drive the second truck.

He extended his hand. "So, you are the dog guy?" He didn't sound like he meant it in a bad way. And to be truthful I would not have cared anyway. I was now inside the security perimeter of some of Her Majesty's finest. I was safe and that's all that mattered.

"Yup, that would be me."

"Can we have a selfie?" That surprised me.

"Yeah of course." We posed for the photo and before I knew it, a short line had formed for a selfie with the Dog Guy.

I watched a curious scene unfold. A long wavering single-file column of young Afghans, men and women, snaked past me and back towards the Taliban-held side of the airport approach.

No one spoke. They carried no bags or possessions I could see, just the clothes on their back. A contingent of British and American soldiers escorted them as they were led to the checkpoint crossing. The coalition soldiers stopped on our side of the barbed wire no man's land as the young people filed back into the Taliban's Afghanistan.

I asked what was occurring.

No one answered.

As the sun dipped behind numerous empty aircraft hangars our little convoy of two trucks was directed into a larger empty hangar of our own, just to the side of the hard standing of northern Kabul airport. As I drove the lead truck into the shadows of the vast structure and parked, I was immediately struck by the mounds of rubbish mixed with discarded clothing and empty suitcases, hundreds of them.

I dismounted from the cab but before I could take a closer look, the major who had greeted me when I had first crossed over from Taliban country to this piece of little England called for me to come over. He'd been the one to drive the second truck.

"Here are the rules, ok?" he asked, waiting for my confirmation.

"Shoot, boss."

"No tweeting and just remain here until your aircraft arrives, ok?"

I smiled. No tweeting. Of all the things I could do and the British military were worried about my use of social media. That's one powerful little tool I had in my pocket. "Staying here is fine with me." I glanced over toward a pile of untouched Italian military rations. Dinner was taken care of for sure.

He nodded his relief. As he spoke, a six-man section of paratroopers all walked into the hangar. They looked worn out. One even sported a ripped sleeve on his combat shirt from the shoulder down to the elbow. I watched the lads unroll their sleeping mats and stretch out. I would have been amazed if they weren't asleep by the time myself and the major had finished our brief conversation.

I immediately went back to surveying the abandoned warehouse. This must have been where refugees were housed whilst they waited to be processed. As they were brought forward to leave, I assumed they were told to ditch their personal possessions.

Once abandoned, the next tranche of refugees would enter the hangar, rifle through the abandoned belongings and just as before, were told to leave their possessions behind.

I bent down and gently picked up a grainy photo. It reminded me of the photos in my mum's family album that was stored in her bedroom wardrobe, stuffed full of the same grainy type of photos taken of our family in the seventies and eighties.

The photograph depicted a mother, kneeling sideways on top of a large white cushion on the floor, her jet-black hair-styled in the disco-dance-queen look of the seventies. I assumed the young man kneeling next to her, facing directly at the camera, was her son. He had a try-hard moustache and bushy dark hair. A younger girl, with long black hair to her waist sat alongside her brother. All looked content and happy.

As I stared at the photo, I wondered what had become of those people. As I looked up and scanned the vast piles of abandoned belongings, mixed with discarded water bottles and military ration pack wrappers, I saw a huge photo album. A family's whole history now lost forever.

Deeper into the hangar was clearly an area that had been used for sleeping, hundreds of military roll mats and cot beds littered the floor.

I picked one up and carefully carried it back to where the trucks were parked, trying my best not to make too much noise in case I woke the sleeping fireteam. I placed the cot bed by the back of the second truck and lay down. When I awoke about two in the morning, the British soldiers were nowhere to be seen. And bizarrely I noticed I was missing the vehicle registration plates of both trucks. Collector's items I guessed, amused. I didn't need them.

My ringing phone had been the source of the irritating noise that woke me from a deep sleep.

"So, we don't have an aircraft?" I asked, not for the first time.

"Yes, we do," was Nina's response, before adding somewhat quietly, "But it cannot technically land as it does not then have permission to take off again for Tashkent."

"Say that again – why have we not got permission to land in Tashkent for fuck's sake?" I demanded, immediately regretting my tone of voice. I knew Nina was doing everything she possibly could and then some in gaining the required permission to have our flight cleared for every aspect of its journey.

There was no *Arranging an Evacuation Flight for Dummies* we could read. Every moment of this evacuation we had made it up as we went along. And sadly, right now Nina was winging this alone.

I rubbed my filthy right hand through my tangled strands of what I now thought, for me anyway, was quite long hair. The action was uncomfortable as I had to force my hand to 'comb' through the knotted and very unwashed mop of hair currently doing its own thing.

My fingers finally won the fight but not without some wincing. The temporary self-inflicted pain woke me up.

I looked across at the two overloaded stationary trucks. There was hardly a noise from any of the plastic crates and the darkened hangar interior made it difficult to see the occupants of the crates anyway.

I sighed heavily. This was my tenth day of operating on three hours or so of sleep per night. Maybe it was finally taking its toll, I mused.

Focus, I scolded myself. Work the problem of how you get out of here. Getting angry at the very person going above and beyond was not helping to create a positive outcome.

I lifted the phone back to my cheek. "Sorry, Nina, not your fault I know. I'm getting frustrated and very tired."

I couldn't understand why we couldn't be given a break just for once. We finally had an aircraft from our fundraising and that alone was a freaking miracle. We should never have been able to achieve that. But the team and our supporters had.

We had won the very public argument between our charity and certain MPs who had put roadblocks up at every possible turn to stop us. The aircraft had permission to land in Kabul. But we now needed permission for it to take-off. How long would the cats and dogs already suffering be able to hold out?

"The plane can take off from Karachi and land in Kabul but... it then cannot depart from Kabul as currently we do not have diplomatic clearance from the authorities in Tashkent for it to land so you can change aircraft," Nina explained patiently. Her voice was quiet. I realised she sounded like she had let me down. She obviously hadn't.

It seemed the whole of our campaign boiled down to a diplomatic endeavour we hadn't thought of. Perhaps we should have. But we were desperate charity workers operating under short notice, not government officials with expertise in international flight procedures – especially not those in a rapidly evolving warzone.

The aircraft coming from Karachi was not a long-haul aircraft. This meant its fuel payload would only support us flying from Kabul to Uzbekistan, just over an hour's flight, where we were then going to have to change to a much larger aircraft with the fuel capacity to reach London. Plus, there was the added complication of insurance. A Western carrier landing in Kabul would have required a hefty insurance premium. It's highly doubtful any broker would have provided it.

To facilitate this evacuation, our aircraft broker had been extremely imaginative. He had used a lesser-known carrier registered in a developing-world country where, I assumed, insurance requirements for landing in a warzone was not as stringent. Once it had delivered us safely to Tashkent then we could use a Western-registered carrier that would have no issues landing in Uzbekistan. British airlines flew daily from London in fact.

However, right now we were still no closer to a solution for landing permission in Tashkent, Uzbekistan.

"Fuck me!" I screamed into the hangar. I wanted to throw my phone into the darkness and listen to the satisfying smash it would make as it collided with the concrete floor. But I parked my anger. Destroying my phone in a fit of rage would have been a rather self-defeating exercise.

"Ok, what do we need to do now?" I asked heavily.

"I'll give you some phone numbers to start calling," was her response.

28 August 2021

I considered ringing Nina for another update. But with Kabul three and a half hours ahead I knew I needed to wait before I gave her a call. Besides, if Nina had secured the required permissions for the aircraft to land, she would have called me immediately. Of that I was dead certain. So I was back to waiting. But now at least I was inside the airport.

Ripped plastic sheeting, now flapping in the slight breeze, was tied to parts of broken fencing all along the outer side of the hangar. Improvised as divides or shelters, I could only imagine the chaos of families attempting to take haven from the harsh sun and garner some sort of privacy whilst waiting for their allocated flights to safety. I left my phone on the camping chair. The charging lead connected to the solar charger I had brought with me was powering up nicely in the glorious morning sun.

Then a *beep beep* and the gunning of a diesel engine. I spun around and immediately recognised the familiar yellow colour of a JCB digger as it slammed its bucket loader into the ground. The driver throttled the engine and what looked like a brand new JCB tractor powered forward, scooping the tossed empty plastic bottles forward as the driver made a pile with the enormous front bucket.

I looked on stunned. "What the fuck?" I said slowly in the direction of the tractor's driver. He was deftly building a pile, reversing the tractor at speed, and then ploughing forward, headlong into the trash, scooping it towards the mini mountain of garbage.

I was more than intrigued.

As I reached the entrance to the hangar, I could see that

the operator of the JCB had by now several substantial mounds of garbage, mostly empty water bottles, forming nicely in the open area. Trails of clear concrete, that I am guessing looked like corn circles if viewed from above, sliced through the discarded trash from the thousands of people forced to flee. The driver was not taking his time. He seemed on a mission as he hurriedly went about clearing the forecourt.

I walked around to the open side window of the digger. The driver was fully kitted up in his military uniform, body armour, and helmet. His assault rifle was clearly leant up against the opposite window of the cab. I could tell he was a Marine by the unit patch on his shoulder, probably in his early twenties.

Before he could engage the gear stick, I yelled up, "What are you doing?" realising as soon as I said it that it sounded dumb. He was clearing rubbish. I could see that. What I had meant to ask was why?

"Clearing garbage," was the honest reply. I smiled back at him. I deserved that answer.

"No, sorry," I shouted, "I meant, why are you clearing the garbage?" Meaning: why was the United States military wasting time cleaning up an airport they were about to hand over to the Taliban?

He looked tired. He leant down towards me so he didn't have to shout. "Commanding officer wants all this cleared up so the Taliban can't accuse us of leaving the airport trashed when we hand it over. I came to fucking Afghanistan to clean trash for the Taliban," he added, clearly not impressed. And who would be?

Of all the current issues surrounding the coalition withdrawal from Afghanistan, some commander somewhere was fretting about what the Taliban would say on their walk around the airport once we'd all gone? And whilst the young serviceman driving the machine was doing a grand job it would take a dedicated work party of hundreds of people to get this place anywhere near decent.

"That sucks," I responded, and it did, big time. Flying thousands of miles to clean crap for the Taliban must have been demoralising.

He nodded and threw the digger into gear. I stepped back as he reversed and turned the wheels slightly to line up a new potential pile of waste to be cleared.

I walked back towards my camping chair. I was still in disbelief at the stupidity of everything.

The next hour or so passed slowly by as I sat watching the digger trundle about the expanse of rubbish, making nice evenly-spaced piles around my frontage. I hardly heard a murmur from within the crates. The dogs and cats were silent. Trying to conserve energy and probably dehydrated. I was wracked with guilt for them but, as with everything else, what else could I do?

It was the smash of glass that startled me. Followed by another and then the thud of something heavy against metal.

It took me a few seconds to orientate to the location of the noise. It was coming from towards the front of my truck. The dogs, woken by the noise, immediately started to bark in distress. The hangar became a cacophony.

I sprinted to the front of the two parked trucks. A United States Marine, huge in stature, dressed in plain olive drab camos, was wielding a pickaxe handle, minus the actual metal head, ready for another swing towards my headlights.

"STOP!" I yelled. "My trucks." I approached him carefully; he still had the wooden handle raised.

"Who are you?" he asked, devoid of emotion. As he said it, I noticed the commotion behind him. Hundreds of Marines were moving around the SUV carpark, vandalising every vehicle they encountered.

I had no time to explain what I really doing there. "Sergeant Farthing, Royal Marines. I am authorised to have these two trucks. Please walk away," I said in as authoritative a way as I possibly could.

"Oh, okay. Sorry, Sergeant," he responded as he lowered the handle. He looked around for something else to smash.

Outside it was full-on smash-up. US Marines versus parked SUVs. I watched as a group of ten Marines heave-hoed a huge white truck up and down like it was a seesaw before it finally rolled onto its roof with a smashing of glass as the windscreen imploded. Not content with that, the Marines set about slashing the tyres.

"What the fuck is going on?" I asked incredulously at the scene unfolding before me.

He stopped looking around and stared at me. "Our commanding officer told us to let off steam," he replied as if that was answer enough.

"Er, ok..." I responded, none the wiser, "Can I ask why?"

"You hear about the suicide bombing at the Abbey Gate?" he asked.

"Yes, yes I did," I answered. I was not about to try and explain I had been caught in the aftermath of it.

"Our guys," he said as he looked down at the ground. The emotion was welling up in his face, "Our friends." The anguish was raw.

I knew only too well the anger and loss felt when one of your own is killed by the enemy. But we had consoled our lads and talked it out. Never had we set them loose on a hooligan rampage like this. This was fucking madness.

I reached out and touched his arm.

"Truly sorry, mate," I said sincerely, "But the trucks are mine, ok?" He nodded his head and turned to look for something else to smash in the hangar. I stood guard as the Marines, eyes glazed with rage and hurt, started to head in my direction.

I won't lie. I felt somewhat apprehensive. If mob mentality ruled, I couldn't defend the trucks.

Off to my left I heard the Marine I had just chatted with take his axe handle to the light switch control box of the hangar.

It was just unreal.

I leant against the bonnet of the truck with my arms folded and tried my best to look hard as the hordes of Marines used the hangar to transit either side of the trucks to reach the open area to the front. I nodded at them all and just spoke clearly to the group at intermittent intervals, "Not the trucks, fellas, they're mine."

Random smashing sounds came from around the hangar as individuals found something they thought of value to wantonly destroy.

The dogs were going crazy, howling and barking as the Marines filed past. Only one, a sergeant, his ranking patches on his arm the giveaway, stopped and looked over at me.

"Working dogs?" he enquired as he attempted to stare into the nearest crate.

Some were, as they came from the embassies we'd had

contracts with. For simplicity's sake I answered, "Yes, I'm trying to get them out of here before everything goes to shit." Although it seemed it already had.

It seemed to be the answer he was looking for. "Good." Then he went on. I guess he had more things to smash. The final Marine finished ripping off the bumper of a white SUV, parked slightly in front of me and then hurried to join his comrades.

The loud boom that echoed through the hangar from behind me, impulsively made me jump. "What the hell now?" I turned to investigate.

The JCB was burning. Black smoke funnelled into the sky. Cheering jubilantly, the Marines stood around the tractor admiring their handiwork.

"You have to be fucking kidding me," I said flabbergasted to the back of the last Marine as he jogged out across the now-cleared area to rejoin his team. In disbelief I yelled, "It's your JCB!" to the group burning it to smithereens. They ignored my yells. And besides it was too late anyway. The cab was completely engulfed.

I was truly speechless. Off to my left a section of Marines had splintered from the team that had surrounded the smouldering JCB and were now currently kicking the shit out a row of porta-johns. Most were lying on their sides, and I could only imagine the hideous scene now to be found inside.

Never in my military career of over twenty years would I have envisioned what I saw that day. These Marines had been through hell and back. And so had our guys too. More than once. But never had we resorted to a rampage like this. It was bloody terrifying to be honest.

Resigned to watching the ongoing destruction, I found an

unopened water bottle and took a hearty swig as I dumped myself down in my camping chair. The spectacle lasted a good hour as the Marines moved away from me and entered an unoccupied prefab office building complex. As the dense black smoke rose in plumes from the burning JCB, I guessed it was probably a hazard to incoming and departing aircraft. Clearly somebody high up the chain of command agreed with me and made a call as not long after the Marines departed, the fire brigade arrived.

And it was not just any fire truck. It was a *fire* truck. A proper red and shiny one. Just like in the movies. Think "Backdraft" with Kurt Russell and William Baldwin. Pulling to a stop a tactical distance away from the JCB, the military fire crew made quick work of extinguishing the smouldering mess.

I had an idea.

I waved at the crew as they prepared to depart. The tallest of them, who I assumed was the team leader as he had seemed to do most of the directing during what was clearly a routine call out, waved back. I stood in preparation to walk over. I was saved the task. He and another of the team had already begun to walk in the direction of the hangar.

"Nice job, fellas," I offered as they arrived, and we shook hands. Both cut a dashing image with their all-American hero looks, kitted out in combat fatigues, body armour and assault rifles. They most definitely looked the part, and could have featured as the centrefold for the annual fireman's calendar.

"Thanks," came the reply. "Hey, you're that dog guy!" It wasn't a question, more a point of order.

I nodded. "Yes indeed, that's me."

"My mom told me about you, she said you're all over the

news back home." I was surprised, although I suppose I had been on a few late-night US talk shows in the previous few days. "Good job, brother." He sounded genuine, and I appreciated the compliment.

The fire truck had now pulled to stop, and the remainder of the crew had dismounted. Some were milling about peering into the crates.

"I could do with some help," I said without really knowing if my idea would work.

"Shoot," was the simple response as he waited for my actual request.

"Any chance you can help to get some water into these crates?" I was desperate to water the dogs and cats but could only realistically get to the outside crates using individual 500ml bottles of water. I eyed the fire truck. "Can you make it rain?" I enquired with the biggest grin I could muster.

"Hell yeah, we can do that," he said with an equally big smile back.

For the next hour the fire crew made it rain inside the hangar, ensuring every crate received a supply of fresh water, especially the inaccessible crates barricaded into the middle of the flatbed.

I am not overly convinced that the dogs and cats enjoyed the water delivery method, but it was the best I could do. I hadn't envisioned I'd be on my own at this stage of the evacuation. I had relied on the Nowzad staff being along for the ride.

No moment of triumph is complete without the compulsory group selfie. We lined up behind the rear truck and with me in the middle, set the ten second timer and took some snaps.

I shook hands vigorously with each of them in turn whilst thanking them profusely for their time. I have no doubt their kindness helped save the animals' lives.

I watched the fire truck pull away, still slightly slackjawed as to how the last few hours had unfolded. I had for a while, forgotten just how dire my situation was. Still nothing from Nina on when, or even if, our aircraft was coming in. And then if by some miracle it did, I was still none the wiser on just how I was meant to load 102 crates into the aircraft hold on my own.

The random events had been enough for one day. It was time for me to start figuring my next move. The noise of an approaching vehicle caught my attention, and I poked my head outside to investigate.

"Ok, this is just weird," I said to the dogs lying quietly behind me in their crates. And it truly was becoming over-the-top weird, as this time a hearse pulled up outside the hangar. A proper black and shiny hearse.

28 August 2021 (Continued)

The dark dot was growing bigger, and that dot was now definitely an aircraft. And it was coming in to land. Was this actually our aircraft? Nobody had exactly gone out of their way to tell me it was and as I looked around, I saw absolutely zero interest in the aircraft coming into land.

There hadn't been a plane in four hours. Throughout that long day of waiting, less than a dozen had arrived and taken off. You wouldn't have known there was an evacuation going on or that people were desperate to escape. The Berlin Airlift in 1948 saw a plane land and take off once every thirty seconds. Yet here I was seventy-three years later during a crisis evacuation and about ten planes landed in the twenty-four hours I waited at the airport.

This whole spin by the government on how everyone was doing their best to evacuate British citizens and entitled Afghans felt like a con.

The side-on profile of the approaching aircraft started to blend into the rapidly darkening silhouette of the mountains that defined the boundaries of Paghman province to the west. I strained hard to keep the aircraft in my line of vision as it turned to make its final approach.

'Oh well,' I said to nobody in particular. I ran to the edge of the airfield and held my arms aloft towards the sky and waved at the aircraft like I was a loon.

I doubted very much anybody was going to take the effort to run over and yell at me for my efforts. And what were they going to do? Ban me from the airport? Within twenty-four hours the US military would abandon the country and the Taliban would be swarming all over this airport. I waved harder.

Nothing happened.

I was now over 100 metres onto the pan and jumping up and down whilst waving my arms around, hollering, "Over here for fuck's sake!" Not a single person anywhere on that airfield was even slightly bothered. The thought crossed my mind that I could be attempting to wave over an aircraft designated for a different interest group. I had no idea. I was going on Nina's prompt. Her last text had said "aircraft inbound".

And then it started a slow deliberate turn. Towards me. "Fucking yes!" I exclaimed. A stupid big grin had broken out on my face. The aircraft was headed toward me and the spot I had designated as our parking bay on this evacuation airfield.

I remembered the strict upright position my arms should be in from my days of marshalling Chinooks. That had always ended up with me being battered into a crouch position as the downdraft of the forward rotor blades of the helicopter whipped up the loose stones and mud and battered me senseless.

As the most beautiful sight of our chartered aircraft approached, I began to bring my arms towards the top of my head in a come-to-me signal. "Oh yeah baby, come to me!" I yelled to absolutely nobody.

Within minutes the tip of the aircraft's nose was within 100 feet of me. The noise was something else. And clearly, I was not wearing ear defenders.

I crossed my arms above my head to signal that was close enough. I became somewhat apprehensive as to whether the pilot was even paying attention to the non-uniformed nutter flapping his arms away stood on the edge of the runway.

"That's close enough, buddy," I mouthed towards the

cockpit. I couldn't actually see the pilots behind the glass windshield of the cockpit. The last thing I wanted was to be run over by the aircraft designated to rescue me. The press back home would have had a field day.

I prepared to bail sideways. Aircraft truly look extremely menacing when bearing down on top of you.

As the pilot applied the brakes and the engines idled, I took a moment to turn around and look towards the road which was slightly higher than the aircraft parking apron. Surely there must be some US Marines idly stood waiting apron-side for their flight home who were somewhat intrigued by what had just happened. After looking left and right along the line of at least 500 uniformed personnel I can safely say, no, not even one showed any interest in me marshalling in a passenger aircraft. Truly surreal.

I gave the thumbs up to the media officer who had stayed with me, although he had been called to form up for 16 Air Assault's departure. Jumping in the first cab of the animals' lorry, I drove it onto the runway and parked the truck twenty feet from the aircraft. The media officer followed me, driving the second truck.

He dropped down from the cab and we shook hands. He wished me luck and jogged off to attend the parade for his chalk to leave Afghanistan. As I turned back to the aircraft, waiting for me was the pilot or maybe the co-pilot (we never had time for proper introductions).

"Guessing you are Dog Guy," he yelled above the noise of the engines. He had a huge smile, and from his accent I was guessing he was from somewhere in Africa but where to be precise I had no idea.

"That I am," I replied. I was beyond happy to see him,

the palpable desire to hug him was almost overpowering. But instead, we shook hands, as you do.

"Let's get loaded, shall we?" he suggested, gesturing to towards the hold.

I followed him as we walked under the belly fairing of the aircraft. He reached up on tiptoes and pulled a lever, revealing an opening in the smooth hull of the aircraft no bigger than a few metres either way.

I just stared at it for a few seconds. The issue wasn't the reduced opening but the fact it was at least six foot off the ground.

"Oh shit," I said.

He then reached up and unfolded a small step ladder which had been placed just inside the opening. That made the opening a whole two foot nearer.

I looked at him and then at the six-foot-high hatch, the step ladder borrowed from the Oompa-Loompas, and then at the two trucks containing 102 crates.

It would take two of us an hour at least just to unload the crates from the trucks.

I stood, not saying a word. I needed a miracle.

This was not the aircraft we had designed our load plan around. For a second, I thought about calling Nina to ask where the original aircraft was. The one that we had planned and trained to load according to an expert's detailed advice. But that thought quickly passed. It wasn't as if this one would take off and I could wait happily for a bigger replacement to arrive.

When everything is going south and odds are stacked up against you, there are two choices in this world. Crack on or curl yourself up in a ball and wait for the world to end. Fight or flight.

I decided to fight.

"Best we get loading then," I yelled as I walked toward the first truck.

From the shocked look on his face, I reckon he had just worked out the enormity of the task ahead of us too. As I started to release the tail gate on the first truck to start the unloading process, I was distracted by the sound of a quickly approaching vehicle. I glanced around the side of the truck to see a sight for sore eyes.

"YES!" I shouted at the night sky. "YES!"

The hearse screeched to a halt in front of the second truck and out piled a group of steely-eyed motherfuckers ready to get some hard graft in loading dogs and cats into a waiting turning-and-burning aircraft.

The day before, after the fire engine had departed, I had assumed nothing else could make my time at this airport any weirder. How wrong I had been.

The arrival of the hearse was the icing on a very unexpected cake. As soon as I saw them clambering out of the vehicle, I knew they weren't regular military unit soldiers. Out of the six who gathered around me no one wore standard military issue clothing.

"Dog Guy, right?" the oldest of the team asked me in his southern American accent. He was clearly also the one in command.

"Yup, Dog Guy," I replied.

We all shook hands as the team wandered off to look at the dogs through the tiny gaps in the sides of the crates, leaving me to chat with their squad leader. It transpired they were Special Forces and had attended the immediate aftermath of the suicide bombing two nights before. They dealt with horrors

I cannot even begin to describe as some of the first on scene.

I dashed to the front of the cab to retrieve a sleeping Ewok from his crate. The little furball quickly became a positive interaction for the emotionally charged lads. He played his role well – almost as if he was a fully certified therapy dog.

I returned to chat with the team leader, who admitted it had been his mum back home in Texas who had told him about a dog guy and had ordered him to aid me if he could. At the time he had humoured her. But when he found out I really was in the airfield he had driven over. Special Forces were a law unto themselves. He didn't have to answer to anyone on this camp.

I chuckled as he told me. And then I asked him for some manpower.

And he had been only too happy to offer the services of his team. In his words, "It will be our pleasure, man, to do something positive from the mess of this fucking shitshow."

Have you ever played Tetris? Your mission is to move and, if required, rotate the shapes so that they form complete rows along the bottom. Fail to complete and it's game over.

Well, I was now playing Tetris in the hold of the Boeing aircraft sent to evacuate me and the animals. Unable to stand in the confined space, I was forced into an uncomfortable crouch to push the crates into position, dragging them backwards towards the aft of the hold. With no plan either, I was making it up as I went along. I would stick my head out, half hanging upside down and pointing frantically at the crate I assumed would fit in the next slot I had available. The curvature of the aircraft's fuselage meant that some crates were jammed in, balanced at a forty-five-degree angle. But the sheer volume of crates being secured in the hold ensured each crate was jammed tight.

I longed for a break to stand up straight and take a breather. Sadly, there was no time for that. We were against the clock.

"How can we help?"

I popped my head down and out of the hold and was surprised to be face to face with a group of female Marines dressed in desert cam who had run over from the side of the runway.

"Cats?" one of the SF team suggested as he pushed past them to lift another crate into the waiting opening. Even the SF guys looked like they could do with a few minutes to catch their breath.

I glanced over at the numerous cat crates stacked randomly on the side of the runway. We didn't have time for me to play Tetris all evening.

"Main cabin please, Marines," as I pointed to the cat crates. "Oorah," I added just for fun.

And with that, the female fireteam set off on their mission to load as many cat crates as they could into the empty seats of the main cabin. "We might as well," I thought to myself. It's not like we had any passengers to fill them, was it?

These are WhatsApp messages directly from Nina's phone on the 27th of August as I had entered the airport, to the Foreign Commonwealth and Development Office contact we had (I have changed the FCDO contact's name to Sarah):

[27/08/2021 18.36.39] Nina: Sarah — please could you send this on ASAP. Nowzad has a charter aeroplane departing from Kabul International Airport

with seats onboard for approximately 100 people.
We would like to help the Foreign Office to give
those people stranded at KIA a seat to the UK.
Please call to discuss further if needed.

[27/08/2021 18:38:31] Sarah: Will pass on.

Once more nothing came of it. Again, nobody responded. This was the third time we used an official contact to send through an offer that evacuees could take up the spare seats available in our aircraft. I had also offered the seats in person as I had arrived at the airport.

Now I realise that for the British government to accept our seats would most likely been seen as a negative. It could be construed as a government failure because it used the seats offered by a "pet" charity to finish the evacuation. My take on it was that ensuring no evacuees took up those spare seats guaranteed the headline would be *Pen Farthing leaves as the only passenger on a chartered flight with his dogs. Seats that could have been used to evacuate desperate interpreters.* And funny old thing... that was the headline in some papers.

It kept up the distraction from the government's incompetency. As I saw it, it made no difference whether cats occupied the empty seats or not.

Forty minutes later, very tired and sweaty, I dropped down out of the hold. There was no space capacity in the cramped interior of the hold. I even had crates on top of crates. I didn't care. The dogs and cats were taking a one-way ticket out of Dodge and that was all I cared about.

The pilot never commented on my loading ability. He just closed the hold's hatch and said we needed to leave.

I shook hands with the SF team and the Marines, and

thanked them from the bottom of my heart for their assistance.

–

The lights from Kabul disappeared rapidly from view through the small cabin window as we gained altitude. I closed my eyes and held Ewok closer.

Elation, sadness, anger, relief all swept over me like a tidal wave. The dogs and cats were safe, but not the staff. All I could do was hope beyond hope that our overland plan worked. There was no other way.

Fifteen years of punishing hard work was over. Everything we had painstakingly achieved was nothing more than historical pages on a website.

As I sat staring into space, my mind wandering through all the possibilities and what-ifs, I was wrenched back into the moment by the air stewardess.

"Would you like some food?" She held a grey plastic tray in her arms. She looked around at the cat crates strapped into the passenger seats behind me. I realised the smell was quite bad. The crates need cleaning.

"Yes please." I couldn't recall the last time I'd eaten. Some time ago for sure.

She placed the tray on the fold down table. I had to laugh. It was a McDonald's, still in the wrapper. Where they had brought that from is anyone's guess.

"Don't suppose you have a beer by any chance, do you?" I asked longingly, and to be honest I was keener for one of those than the food she had served.

"No, sorry, we don't," was her reply and she turned to leave.

I was looking forward to arriving in Tashkent. Dan, the charity chairman, and Ian from the evac committee, were both flying in specially to connect with me during the transfer from this aircraft to the larger one capable of the long-haul flight to England. Ian's skills as a veterinarian were to be utilised to give the animals a once-over. Both would then accompany me to Heathrow.

What I was not expecting was the welcome that awaited me as we landed in Tashkent, capital of Uzbekistan. We taxied for what seemed like ages to a secluded area of the airport where, to my surprise, a squad of brown-uniformed troops carrying AK-47 rifles surrounded the aircraft.

"Well, that's a bit much," I said to Ewok as I lifted him so he could look out the window at the line of armed soldiers. I wasn't overly sure why they were there. I had no intention of trying to escape. I just wanted to go home.

Nothing happened for nearly an hour. From text messages with Dan, I deduced they were both lost in the main Tashkent terminal, unable to find officials willing or with any knowledge of how they would transit to the secluded area of the airport where we were parked.

I got frustrated from the wait to disembark. So I walked through the main cabin of the aircraft and into the closed business-class section. I found the pilot and flight crew relaxing there, happily chugging on bottled beers and two of the stewardesses even sharing a bottle of wine.

With a look of disdain, I nodded at the stewardess who had told me they had no beer onboard. She was not going to be on my Christmas card list.

It transpired the crew had no idea what was going on either. No officials from Tashkent had come onboard yet. And so, I went back to start checking on the cats. I was extremely keen to just get going. It was then that I made a dreadful, gruesome discovery.

Six of the crates contained dead cats. I have no idea when they died and for a while, I felt horribly guilty I hadn't checked on them sooner. But as pointed out to me by Ian when he finally arrived, I had no ability or time to check on them before now. And what could I have done? I was no veterinarian and had no medical supplies with me even if I was.

The six dead cats I wrapped carefully into black bin bags. I wasn't going to just trash them and leave them on the aircraft. They would be coming back with us. The autopsy back in the United Kingdom found the cats had died from severe irritation to their windpipe and lungs. Basically, the long-term effects of the tear gas. We assumed that the tear gas, as it sticks to clothes, had done the same to the fur of the cats. And cats lick their fur to keep it clean. Horrifically, they had been continually ingesting tear gas. It was the black shadow cast by the horror of the evacuation, and a bitter end to its success.

Finally, after what seemed like forever, a minibus arrived, and Dan and Ian had clambered up the back steps to greet me. It was so good to see friendly faces.

After a quick catch up we set about unloading the cats from the cabin into neat rows on the tarmac. This was now a game of Tetris in reverse. I truly believe it was harder lifting the crates down and out of the hold than it was lifting them up.

We carefully cleaned a few crates where the dogs had been unable to hold it in, which was not surprising as they had been locked in their crates for nearly thirty-six hours.

Dan carefully held the dog, wrapped securely in his arms whilst I took on the fun job of cleaning the crate. Dan's perks of being the chairman, I guess.

In the end it was another good two hours before the new aircraft arrived that would be our ark for the next phase of the journey to England. And thankfully somebody within the airport management saw fit to provide a crew to assist with the loading.

29 August 2021

I hadn't seen a single air hostess since they had served breakfast a few hours ago. With both Dan and Ian sleeping soundly in business class I was alone with the cats in economy.

I smirked. It was either now or never as this opportunity wasn't going to come along again. As the wing tip crossed the western boundary fence of the east–west runway I unfastened my seat belt.

The naughty schoolboy took over and I seized one last guilty look up and down the cabin to ensure that there was no air hostess sneaking up on me to spoil my fun. Happy that the coast was clear, I pushed out into the aisle.

Adopting the stance of a surfer, arms outstretched I used the tension in my leg muscles to ride through the landing, balanced in the aisle. As the cabin was jolted by the wheels of the aircraft contacting the runway at around 160 miles per hour, I let out a "YEAH!" and waved my hands in the air. I did a little dance – nobody was watching, and I didn't care if they were anyway.

I was home! Back on British soil.

Against everything thrown at us, I had landed in London with the dogs and cats. And if all went well with our revised plan, then our staff would be on their way through Jalalabad and south east to the Torkham crossing into Pakistan soon enough.

I gave another whoop.

I looked around at the rows of empty seats. Sadness replaced my elation at being home. They should have been filled with our staff or desperate people fleeing the carnage left behind by the withdrawing coalition.

I needed to find decent internet capabilities and get caught up on where Nina and the team were with arranging the overland trip to the Pakistan border crossing.

Thankfully, I didn't have to wait long before the aircraft doors were crosschecked and opened, and an influx of official-looking folks in hi-vis vests accompanied by two heavily armed police officers, their Heckler & Koch MP5 rifles strapped across their chests in the ready position, boarded the flight.

I immediately thought that everybody just looked so damn serious.

"Okay, you three with these officers," said one of the airport officials indicating to myself, Dan, and Ian as we stood between a row of seats amongst the cats. I asked, "What about the dogs and cats?"

It was suddenly dawning on me that I was no longer in control.

"They will be dealt with by animal services," was the somewhat irritated-sounding reply.

"Okay." I smiled directly at him and held his gaze. "This is an evacuation flight my friend, I have cats doubled up in crates, some dogs are three to a crate and a few," I knew this would freak him out before I said it, "that we had to cram in the galley back there." I pointed aft to the back of the aircraft.

"You've done what?" He sounded incredulous. "Are you kidding me?"

On any other flight arriving at any British airport, dogs and cats being imported would arrive one animal to a crate and secured in the cargo hold. They would then be retrieved by authorised quarantine professionals – however, that only applied when a professional airport team were tasked with loading the aircraft at the originating destination. The fuck-around in Tashkent had meant that I, along with Dan and Ian, had the responsibility of our load plan. And because we didn't have a load plan, we had crammed the dogs and cats that would not fit in the cargo hold into the cabin of the aircraft. It was not like we had any passengers to moan about seats being unavailable. The British government had made sure of that.

"The folks from quarantine will need my help to identify which animals are going where as I believe we are using four different quarantine centres. And yes, we have dogs in crates in the galley area as I had nowhere else to put them. The authorities at Tashkent weren't really that helpful to be honest." Both Dan and Ian nodded in agreement at my last statement, whilst grinning at the official's look of unease.

"But you can't go airside," he blurted out, looking around for confirmation from anyone who had boarded with him.

Until that moment I never really thought through the finer points of airport security and how we are all corralled through a one-way system to finally arrive at immigration. I was now realising I was about to mess up a well-honed system.

A shorter guy with a huge clipboard piped up. "If he is the only person who knows which dogs are where then I need him." I assumed he oversaw animal services and knew the importance of ensuring dogs were allocated to their correct quarantine facility. Due the number of dogs and cats we had evacuated we were even having to take quarantine spaces as far north as Scotland.

"He can't just wander around outside the aircraft on his own," came the worried response from the first official. He looked around for the backup that was not coming his way.

"I'll escort him," came the stern reply from the armed officer. I nodded a thank you to him. "If he tries to escape, I'll shoot him," he added with a smirk. Instantly I liked him. My sense of humour.

The first official shook his head and mumbled, "Okay," but then quickly added, "I want him processed through immigration as soon as the animals are unloaded." And with that he turned and ushered Dan and Ian to grab their belongings and head towards the aircraft door.

The armed policemen bent over toward me so just I would hear what he was about to say. "So fucking glad you stood up to that Wallace dick," he said winking, "the guy's a prat." I just smiled back. It was not for me to deny or confirm. "You did a good thing, Royal," he continued.

"Thank you, I appreciate that," I replied. It meant so much to hear him add "Royal" on the end. Those who have served in the military and respected my service would say that as they greeted a Royal Marine. And I was grateful to know I was not as universally hated as I thought I might be.

–

Living in Afghanistan since the outbreak of the pandemic, I had missed the policies around containing Covid. Even though I had been fully vaccinated with the Indian version of the Astra-Zeneca vaccine and been in proximity with Dan and Ian, I was ordered to spend two weeks in a quarantine hotel at a cost of around £2,000. Yet Dan was free to catch the next flight to Texas, and Ian had called a taxi to go straight home.

After what I had just been through there was no way I was going to be isolated in an eight-foot by eight-foot room for two weeks. Not a chance.

"I am going home," I gleefully replied, "but to Norway and my wife." I was all smiles. I just needed a transfer to Terminal Two and my British Airways flight, fully paid for courtesy of The Daily Mail in return for an exclusive interview once I arrived.

The official laughed. "Fair enough, when is the flight?"

The operational management team that handled me at Heathrow airport was bloody marvellous, pulling out all the stops to transport me from Terminal Four to Terminal Two so I could directly board my Oslo-bound flight, happily bypassing most other passengers along the way.

Restricted areas and security checkpoints were transited with ease, which even allowed time for a quick stop in a business lounge en route so I could grab that long-awaited beer. I chugged the first one in probably three gulps, hardly touching the sides as it went down the hatch. Yeah. It tasted damn good.

As I boarded, I really felt sorry for the person booked into the seat next to me on the hour-long flight to Oslo. I knew I stank. I hadn't changed my clothes in nearly five days of forty-degree heat.

Again, Covid rulings as I arrived in Oslo just did not make sense. Kaisa had received her vaccine the same time as I had in Kabul at the same clinic, yet when she arrived in Oslo after meeting her mum in front of all local and national TV cameras, she was allowed straight home. Whereas I, as a British citizen, had to undergo a form of quarantine. I guess local nationals don't transmit Covid like us Brits do.

But the silver lining was that it was only for three days in a hotel, and I had my bag of clean clothes specially packed from Kabul that I had brought with me. That first shower was going to be truly amazing. And the Norwegian government had seen fit to allow outdoor exercise for all quarantined individuals. I was longing to go for a run, really stretch my legs.

"Let's go," the Norwegian Chief Covid Escort said.

"My bag has not arrived yet," I indicated toward the empty baggage carousel. It was ridiculous that we were off to a quarantine hotel yet here we were, mixing with everyone in the packed baggage reclaim area.

The escort told me to stay put whilst he led a group who had already been reunited with their hold baggage to the quarantine hotel processing area adjacent to the baggage reclaim.

Now was my chance I decided, as I was left alone staring at an empty carousel. The duty-free shopping for arrivals at Oslo airport was located within the same hall as the rows of baggage reclaim belts. No way I was being holed up in a hotel room on my own for three days without any booze.

I trotted off to find some red wine and a bottle of rum.

If the escort noticed the obvious white duty-free bag propped by my foot when he returned, he never said anything.

Five days in the same clothes was about to become six and seven respectively as good old British Airways managed to misplace my small bag and the vital change of clothes it contained. At the baggage enquires desk the assistant handed out a small prepacked bag. It contained Y-fronts, a vest, toothbrush, and toothpaste.

And as I left the terminal building to board the bus, there she was.

My shield-maiden. My beautiful Nordic angel.

She was leaning against the simple waist-high metal barrier that separated the general public from the arriving passengers apparently full of Covid. She stood, waiting for me.

Her beautiful smile just became bigger as we clocked each other.

Fuck the rules.

I rushed over to her against the shouts of whatever was being said in Norwegian by my Covid escort.

We hugged and kissed. Her welcome embrace just pure magic. Until that moment I had had no idea whether we would ever see each other again. There was not a single person in the world who was going to take this moment from me. Nothing else mattered. The last few weeks of hell were forgotten.

And then my escort dragged me away.

I had three more days to do in a "loose" quarantine facility. I could handle that knowing my Kaisa was there, waiting for me.

And so that evening, I sat in an oversized pair of Y-front pants and a very baggy vest in the Nordic quarantine room drinking the expensive bottle of red wine I had purchased in duty-free. I remember laughing, crying, and generally going through a whole host of emotions as I sat on my own staring at the brown wall of the small-but-functional room before I passed out on the bed.

As far as I was concerned, the worst was over. We had successfully evacuated the dogs and cats from Kabul, hopefully soon the Nowzad staff and their families would be over the border and into Pakistan, and I was home to Kaisa. I didn't know what would happen next, but it couldn't be worse than what I had just been through.

How wrong I was.

Part 4:
The Price Paid

30 August 2021

I woke up to a firestorm.

While in Afghanistan I'd used social media and mainstream media for three reasons. One was absolutely and unapologetically to get visas for my staff and their families, and permission to land a plane and fly it out again. If you've followed the journey from page one you already know all the hurdles we had to get over.

Another reason was to keep Nowzad followers informed because they cared about our animals and staff. And finally, I used the media to inform the public about what was going on. As the conflict and confusion grew in Kabul, journalists and other English-speaking workers left until there was pretty much just me and a guy from the Sun. So I gave more and more interviews to many media outlets about the situation on the ground as it unfolded that had nothing to do with Nowzad. By the time I landed in Norway, I had given interviews to every newspaper and TV station in Britain, plus many in the USA and around the world.

The media was one of the few tools I had in my kitbag, and I used it to the best of my ability in order to do what I had to do. It was the only way that I could get the government's attention. It got us out of the country and to safety.

But other people have access to it too. And they used it to demonise me and, in the process, to eviscerate the ability of Nowzad to operate effectively. And then, this false narrative got a life of its own.

Here's just one of many examples from many established media persons.

Larisa Brown, defence editor for The Times, posted on

Twitter on the 28th of August 2021 at 8.54pm (UK Local):

> Pen Farthing's flight departed Kabul today with 94 dogs, 74 cats and one human. Defence source said: "Not only did he abandon his Afghan staff, but they loaded up their plane with dogs at the same time as the US were loading up their 13 dead. Everyone here is absolutely broken."

What I don't get is why a respected and influential journalist working in a leadership position at a leading broadsheet used her status as a bullhorn for the government's propaganda without spending any time to see if it was true. I thought that the media were supposed to pursue the truth even if that meant holding the government's feet to the fire. I suppose some clever lawyer-type could defend this as "contributing to the national conversation" and as an example of the 21st century news cycle where journalists have to immediately push out every single bit of info regardless of its veracity.

But from where I was sitting, it sure felt like a smear.

Worse still, this tweet from an unnamed defence source used the murdered thirteen US Marines. I can't grasp why someone would compare the abhorrent toll from a suicide bomber with our evacuation of animals. It's appalling.

By the way, those Marines were given a full military send-off the day I sat around the hangar. Not one US military service member voiced displeasure or hurt that I was evacuating the dogs and cats. All I spoke to, and I spoke to a lot, were quite happy that somebody was looking out for the dogs and cats. I was even asked to pose for a fair few selfies, and as you know some of the US troops kindly volunteered to help me load the kennels into the aircraft. In no way did the Nowzad evacuation impede the American evacuation. And – obviously – my Afghan staff was not "abandoned".

The British military handed over our Lashkar Gah bases in 2014. The British government had seven years to evacuate the staff who worked for us at embassies and other outposts. Yet it didn't. It had eighteen months from the Doha Agreement to put in place a plan to evacuate our people and eligible Afghans. Yet it didn't. The failure to evacuate interpreters, Special Forces, and anyone else who worked for or served alongside British forces in Afghanistan sits squarely with the British government.

I do think it's possible that as the government's failures became evident, it needed a distraction. A bait and switch. In the hope that no one would notice the rank stench of failure, the narrative got flipped from me doing something decent against all odds, to me somehow being a villain putting others' lives at risk.

So lies were dumped on me. Ludicrous accusations or bizarre comparisons, like the murdered US Marines. MPs like Tom Tugendhat said on-air that, "We just used a lot of troops to bring in 200 animals, meanwhile my interpreter's family are likely to be killed." I truly hope the family made it to safety. But what a disgraceful thing to say, as if I was the one responsible for who got out. Not to mention the only troops involved in my case were volunteers from the US military who happened to be there. It was a prime example of scapegoating me for the British government's failures.

It all became a social media mob with a life of its own. My reputation was publicly destroyed whilst I was on the ground attempting to evacuate my staff and later when I was home.

Imagine how easy that would be if I had received a call

during that first week of the evacuation campaign when I was just starting to tweet out my frustration. "Hi Pen, I'm John Doe from the military (or Home Office or FCDO). Let's talk and see if we can come to some arrangement to get you and your staff and your animals out, and in exchange you stop being so vocal."

Then we would have talked civilly and, more than likely, come to some mutually satisfactory arrangement that could have been presented in the British media as a win for both sides.

Instead a "senior Whitehall official" predicted "that the animals will have to be destroyed on arrival" because they were diseased. I've no idea why they said this as it just wasn't true.

I really have an issue now with unnamed officials from any level of the government making unfounded comments. "Where's the proof?" the media should have demanded.

The "senior Whitehall official" hadn't supplied any. These lies weren't harmless. The abuse my staff and I received was real enough. People seemed genuinely happy at the thought that dogs and cats would be killed.

The evacuation didn't have to be shambolic. I didn't have to be writing this book. Governments govern, that's their job. Their job is to protect their citizens (and those who support the citizenry) through solving problems.

Our government didn't. Instead I got blamed for its failures.

For the rest of my life, I will be labelled as the guy who prioritised pets over people.

It fucking sucks. For me. For Nowzad.

On the 23rd of August at 8.32pm (UK Local) or more relevant to me, midnight in Afghanistan, I had sent a voice note to Peter Quentin, policy advisor to Ben Wallace, the Defence Secretary. If you have not heard it, you can Google it. I basically threatened to destroy him if he did not give us the clearance for the flight to escape from Kabul. The voice note lasts one minute and fifty-five seconds and contains too many F-bombs for me to repeat here.

I was angry, very tired, scared, and desperate to get my people and the animals we cared for out of Afghanistan. It was impossible for me to communicate to those in power how terrifying the situation was for those of us on the ground. The Taliban were there, and every second of every day our lives, from the workers to their children, were in danger. And I was at a loss to protect them or save them or even to get the fucking government to recognise the situation.

Peter Quentin became the focus of all that frustration. Reflecting on the whole sorry saga, Peter could have called me, asked me to apologise, which I absolutely would have done. In the shitshow of everything else going on, I immediately forgot about the message. The first I knew of it was when it was leaked.

In any case, Peter didn't call or message again. And neither did I.

Not my best work for sure.

That voice note was later leaked to the press, The Times if I recall, in yet another startling coincidence. It was released to coincide with me landing safely at Heathrow airport with the dogs and cats. Whoever released it did so with the absolute intent to overshadow my successful arrival home. And they most definitely achieved their aim.

In Oslo with the gorgeous Norwegian summer days beckoning outside, I sat in Kaisa's mum's living room, head in hands, whilst I took part in interview after interview, the focus of every one that bloody voice note. I was made to listen to it again and again during live interviews. With the F-bombs bleeped out, it sounded like some weird rap song. "Bleep, bleep, out of Afghanistan, bleep, bleep."

I issued a truthful apology: "I'm incredibly embarrassed about my language, I do apologise to everybody who's listened to that. I was at the lowest point I could possibly be. I understand how the world works but emotions got the better of me, so for all those who had to listen to that I do apologise for my language."

I repeated it interview after interview, hoping that the subject would then change to how our overland evacuation plans for our staff were going. But not once did any interviewer ask about our staff or even the dogs and cats.

My Norwegian in-laws were horrified at the levels of abuse I was receiving from all quarters. They had seen the story of Operation Ark as a tiny positive endeavour against the backdrop of negativity and tragedy surrounding the withdrawal. They believed it was something for Britain to be proud of, not whipping up hatred about.

Once the dust settled from that one, I was lambasted by journalists and military commentators who accused me of having our Nowzad staff prioritised over interpreters as they crossed the border into Pakistan.

So let me restate this:

The UK government never transported the Nowzad staff to the Torkham crossing at the Afghan-Pakistani border. We did.

Our staff was held in the cramped and poorly supplied hotel for five days, a stressful and very dangerous time as Taliban patrols were looking for those attempting to flee the country.

It cost £275,000, money donated by the public to secure the safe evacuation of our staff. To secure their safe passage to a roadside hotel just short of the border crossing itself, we employed a British private security company still able to operate in Afghanistan even though it was under control of the Taliban.

During late 2021, a member of our evac team was even summoned to Westminster to discuss with a sitting MP the use of security teams in Afghanistan.

It was never a secret.

Nina and Sam worked around the clock to finalise the required paperwork for them to legally cross. On standby to arrange the onward travel to Islamabad, we even had a contact, Farid (the adopted son of Dutch Dorothy, all very complicated but they will appreciate the mention).

We had started to plan this move right from the very moment we arrived back in our compound the night of the failed attempt to gain entry to the airport, a full fifteen days before our team were given permission to cross into the safety of Pakistan.

Everything we did was above board and only achieved through sheer determination and perseverance. Never had a mightier team assembled who could get the job done or do it better. I was and still am truly proud of their herculean efforts.

While all this was going on, Nowzad itself was being investigated by the Charity Commission because someone had apparently complained to it. But here's the thing: the Charity Commission website states, "Before submitting a complaint, you must *complain directly to the charity first.*"

Nobody submitted a complaint to us, not a single person. Yes, they called us names, yes, they sent us death threats, but nobody submitted a formal complaint, to which of course, we would have answered in detail.

The commission's letter, dated the 9th of September, simply said:

> It would be helpful to have the trustees' comments on the following:
>
> 1. How the fundraising initiative, Operation Ark, is in furtherance of the charity's objects.
>
> 2. How much Operation Ark has raised, and what the funds have/will be spent on.

This initial letter had no mention of the fact we were being investigated. But two days later, the BBC reported, *Nowzad charity being investigated by the Charity Commission.*

This wasn't just news to the nation. It was news to us. We didn't know we were being investigated or why, or who told the BBC. The reporter told us his sources were "political". I'll just leave that one with you.

We soon realised the BBC were right and there was an investigation into us. Letter after letter arrived, seeking clarification and information to which we painstakingly co-operated fully for almost a year. Some supporters who read we were being investigated wrote letters or emailed us to confirm they were ending their financial support.

I needed a break from the trauma of the evacuation but the fallout was never-ending. Planned evenings of climbing or just having a chilled-out meal in a decent pub somewhere in the Devonshire countryside were often cancelled.

"Sorry Kaisa, I have to attend a meeting with the solicitors and the trustees tonight now because of another fucking letter that arrived." I never even realised my anger or the disappointment in her face as I let her down. "We will make it up tomorrow." But I never kept my promise. Another fire would burn bright, and I was the only one who could put it out.

I was being completely smothered by the fallout from Operation Ark. My life, the charity, and supporting our Afghan staff to resettle was all put on hold whilst I examined and re-studied the commission's questions. The charity's very existence was on the line.

But Kaisa was beginning to drift away.

In July of 2022, the Charity Commission published their conclusions to the investigation which fully cleared us of any wrongdoing. The accusations got the headlines but the truth barely made the news.

But the time and energy we could have spent on something more useful. And the stress. And the misery. And the rage.

–

On the 11th of September 2021 – exactly twenty years to the day of the Twin Towers attacks in America that claimed the lives of sixty-seven British nationals, sixty-seven Afghans (the combined total of the Nowzad staff and their immediate families) crossed into Pakistan to start the journey towards their new lives in Britain.

The numerical coincidence of that was not lost on me. I pulled the pin on a celebratory can of expensive Norwegian lager as I sat in Oslo, staring out the vast living room windows at a glorious tree-covered view towards the northern edge of the suburb of Korsvoll. The relief was overwhelming. The staff were on their way to the British High Commission in Islamabad where they would be taken care of and processed for their onward journey to the United Kingdom.

On the 5th of October 2021 at 0740hrs, Hamida arrived in Heathrow airport. She had cleared immigration and customs and was stood next to the Costa Coffee in the arrival's hall.

She sent me a text:

Hello Pen, I am in England.

I stood up and cheered.

–

It took over two months but they are all here now. And in fact two of our Afghan team have visited me while I've been writing this book for an afternoon of tea and shortbread biscuits. None of them felt abandoned by me. Very much the opposite.

December 2021 - June 2022

In December 2021, even whilst the Charity Commission's investigation was ongoing, all hell broke loose.

Nearly six months after the events of Operation Ark concluded, the House of Commons Foreign Affairs Select Committee held an Inquiry on Government Policy in Afghanistan. It delved into the chaos of the hastily-led evacuation and revealed some eye-opening turns of events.

One Foreign Commonwealth and Development Office (FCDO) desk officer's submission was the most damning. In its thirty-five pages, it listed the failures: lack of urgency, lack of coordination, lack of planning, assumption that all those who could be evacuated could get into the airport's safe space, ineffectual coordination between ministers and civil servants – it goes on and on and on. The document concluded that fewer than 5% of Afghans who qualified for evacuation actually got evacuated, and some of those left behind were murdered by the Taliban. Every statement was backed up either by his own personal experience or with supportive paperwork.

Bizarrely, he also spewed bald-faced lies about me and the Nowzad evac team. He said that we were part of the problem. He offered no supportive paperwork. And obviously had no personal experience as he was working out of his pleasant office somewhere in England and wasn't in Kabul. He quoted no one. He presented statements as if they were undisputed truths. In fact, they were complete lies.

It's impossible for me to be anything but bitter about the author of this document, Raphael Marshall. He was a wrecking ball in my life – protected by parliamentary privilege.

Everyone who testifies at a select committee gets parliamentary privilege. This means that the person giving testimony cannot be sued for defamation. Which is very useful when you're Raphael Marshall and you haven't a shred of evidence.

So Marshall got dubbed a "whistleblower". He wasn't a whistleblower. He was there at the government's invitation, doing what every government employee should do: help our government perform competently. No kudos from me. As far as I am concerned, he was just doing his job.

Here are two of the 254 paragraphs he submitted as evidence:

213. This is because soldiers tasked with escorting the dogs through the crowd and into the airport would by definition have otherwise been deployed to support the evacuation of British nationals or Afghans prioritised for evacuation, notably by helping families out of the dangerous crowd into the airport. As noted in paragraph 125. the limited number of British soldiers available to help UK visa holders and British citizens from the crowd into the airport was an important limiting factor on our ability to evacuate people.

217. I believe that British soldiers were put at risk in order to bring Nowzad's animals into the airport. It has been reported that British soldiers ventured into the crowd around Kabul airport to clear the way for Nowzad's vehicles. At this point, the crowd was estimated to exceed 25,000 people, with many Taliban fighters present.

There were many reports of people being crushed to death. On 26 August, 13 US Marines and around 170 civilians were murdered by an ISIS-K suicide bomber in the same area of the airport. In these circumstances, any task which involved British soldiers venturing into the crowd presented a meaningful risk to the soldiers.

When he said that, I'd been back for months. Why not contact me? Or the soldiers who'd been there? It's not as if we were invisible or unknown. It's not as if he hadn't had the time to double-check the information.

"How can he just make this stuff up?" I asked Kaisa. I was just stunned.

Not a single British soldier had come outside the wire to assist me. You could spend the rest of your life looking for a soldier who served during Operation Pitting to confirm they came outside the perimeter of Kabul airport to escort dogs through the crowd. You'd be wasting your time. Because not one ever did.

And I never asked them to.

I knew from day one that it was *my* responsibility to secure safe passage for my team and the animals into Kabul airport.

By that evening however, all the major news channels were reporting what Raphael Marshall had said as fact. And since much of the rest of the report was indeed correct, this was a reasonable assumption for the media to make.

But it was an epic disaster for Nowzad and me.

Let me make myself clear. It was not the responsibility of a civilian to organise an effective and humanitarian evacuation of Kabul, nor my fault that it was a disaster. My job was to run an animal welfare charity and care for its staff. End of.

The British government refused to supply the appropriate approvals in time, refused to recognise the reality of running the Taliban gauntlet to get into the airport, and then refused to take responsibility. It was wholly and completely and totally on the government.

The Select Committee's Inquiry on Government Policy in Afghanistan did not ask for my response to Marshall's evidence for over two weeks and, when it did ask, it wanted the response by email. Email. About the accusation that I endangered our soldiers.

By the time my response was published by the inquiry, it was a month later. My comments were never reported.

Soon after, the opposition parties used the whistleblower's testimony to hammer Boris Johnson during Prime Minister's Questions in parliament. The Yorkshire Post on the 27th of January 2022 reported the damning accusation of Dan Jarvis, a former British Army officer and now Labour MP. Mr Jarvis claimed that Nowzad's evacuation had "cost lives".

Imagine being accused of that – of costing someone their life.

Yet I could not challenge what Dan Jarvis said because he too had parliamentary privilege. I had no protection. I had no legal recourse to defend myself and my charity against these deeply offensive accusations. I was just supposed to suck it up. My frustration was from a complete inability to do anything in response.

I went from being a distraction from the government's cockups to being caught in the crossfire between political parties jostling for power. How this affected me or Nowzad was apparently irrelevant. When the establishment turns on even one of its citizens and gets away with it, then it's not good for any of us.

You have no idea how many emails I received that day following Raphael Marshall's report and Dan Jarvis's performance during PMQs.

"I know where you live scumbag – watch your back"
"People like you are just hideous humans; your time will come"

The threats never scared me. But the knowledge that people truly believed that I had caused deaths bothered me beyond belief.

The media piled on. I had wall-to-wall hostile coverage from mainstream media. Here's just one example that was not hostile but ludicrous: The Sun's website has a video, which is still available, depicting the route I took when flying out of Kabul. The aircraft that the newspaper tracked, that I was supposedly in as I made my last-minute escape from the clutches of the Taliban, landed in Muscat in Oman.

I have never been to Oman in my life.

I get it, I know how the world works. Media needs clicks to sell advertising, and I was cannon fodder for the business model.

Nonetheless, I was almost broken by that. That night I opened the first of several bottles of red with the first glass going down around five o'clock. Looking back on it now, I know Kaisa was unimpressed with my coping strategy. I just never saw it at the time.

Good friends, work colleagues, and supporters all told me

to ignore what has been and is being written. Probably good worldly advice. But literally impossible to follow when it is your name being dragged through the mud.

"But that's not what happened," I would respond, completely exasperated. And also, "Why should I just stay quiet?"

Nobody had an answer for me.

–

The House of Commons Foreign Affairs Committee's Inquiry published its findings on the 24th of May 2022 with the title "Missing in Action: UK Leadership and the Withdrawal from Afghanistan" which pretty much says it all really.

This paragraph stood out for me:

> The international withdrawal from Afghanistan has been a disaster in terms of planning, execution, and consequences for the UK's wider interests. It was a betrayal of our partners in the country and, worst of all, undermined the security of the United Kingdom by encouraging our enemies to act against us. The former head of the armed forces told us that the decision to withdraw was 'strategically illiterate and morally bankrupt'.

–

The Foreign Affairs Committee more or less took Raphael Marshall's side on almost everything, finding "systemic failure in terms of strategic planning, policymaking and operational management that is wider than any of the individuals named in this report. We also found a worrying refusal to engage openly with this inquiry, which has damaged our trust in the department."

Why does this matter? Because now that we are involved in Ukraine and tensions around the world are rising, we need to learn from the failures of the Afghan Evacuation. That was the point of the select committee's inquiry. But the elite running our country undermined our ability to do so.

The same select committee also disagreed with Marshall's "facts" about Nowzad. It exonerated Nowzad from any wrongdoing. "We make no criticism of the organisation, its staff, or those who campaigned on its behalf: they were open about their case and objectives, which were in keeping with their stated priorities," the report said.

Lord Tariq of Wimbledon concluded:

"At no point in Op Pitting, therefore, were animals prioritised over people. Our civilian evacuation processing capability, and our military on the ground, were never diverted from evacuating civilians in order to deal with Nowzad's animals."

That went largely unreported. In any case, the die had been cast with me as the villain.

One of my godsons, himself now a Royal Marine, had been undergoing a training course at the Commando Training Centre in Devon, home to all Marines. The instructor never knew that he was related to me. In front of thirty impressionable young Marines, the instructor labelled me a "coward" and "unfit to wear the Green Beret of the Royal Marines" due to my apparent priority of rescuing "pets over people".

When the story had been retold to me, I was devastated. Just numb at the ignorance of one of my own. These young

Marines should have been told I stayed true to the ethos of our Corps by not abandoning my team. Yet now they are in some weird, warped world where I am known as a coward.

One of the reasons why my voice didn't cut through, and neither did the full exonerations from the Charity Commission or the Foreign Affairs Committee, was due to the ongoing media scrum over the role of then-Prime Minister Boris Johnson and his wife, Carrie, in the evacuation. The rumour mill was in overdrive. The press reported on it, and then social media amplified it until it became widely accepted as the truth.

But what really happened had no intrigue whatsoever. Everyone went bananas over nothing.

There is an animal rights activist called Dominic Dyer, a master of social media. He decided to pressure Boris Johnson into admitting he had authorised our evacuation. I asked Dominic several times if he had definitive proof that it was Boris who gave permission. He replied he did not. The pressure on me to reveal what everyone thought I knew was hideous. So I asked him to just stop.

Dyer didn't.

Hand on heart, I knew nothing about the decisions made to authorise Operation Ark from within the British government at the time. And you know what? When you stand in the dust, beyond tired and hungry, the heat bearing down on you, the responsibility of so many people and animals depending on you... you truly don't fucking care who authorised it.

You are just glad somebody did.

In January 2022, it came to a head. The press got a hold of the letter from the 25th of August granting us permission to leave. I received the original letter on the 25th of August, via email, directly from Trudy the MP. It is reproduced below.

Dear Paul,

I am writing to inform you that I have received confirmation from the Foreign, Commonwealth, and Development Office that you, your staff, and their dependents are permitted to travel to The Baron Hotel, Zohak Village, Kabul. You must use the gate entrance on Abbey, also known as Airport Road. You must bring all your passports and documentation.

The Secretary of State has confirmed that a landing slot would be made available for a chartered aircraft to carry yourself, your 68 personnel, and animals in your care. If you do not require a flight for your animals, the Secretary of State has confirmed that a Royal Air Force flight would be made available for all persons.

I have enclosed the personal details of those cleared.

I, therefore, confirm that you should proceed to the airport and wish the very best for your onward journey.

Yours sincerely,
[scrawled signature]
Trudy Harrison MP
Member of Parliament for Copeland
Parliamentary Private Secretary to the Prime Minister

The press went into overdrive. So did the opposition. This apparently was clear proof that Boris Johnson was guilty as charged, that he had approved the flight for personal reasons, and that the approval had not gone through the appropriate process.

The letter went viral as commentators far and wide were tripping over themselves to print the headline that Boris Johnson had authorised the "pets over people" flight.

If Trudy was really working as a proxy for Boris Johnson, then why did it take 'til the 25th of August before we received any confirmation in writing that our team had been called forward to be evacuated? If she really knew that we would be receiving permission to greenlight Operation Ark on the evening of the party, then she has one hell of a future career as an actor when she retires from politics. The reality was that she had just as little an idea of what Boris was going to do as the next person did.

The tragic or funny thing, depending on how you look at it, was that there was absolutely nothing sinister about it.

On the 17th of August 2021, six months before, The News & Star, Cumberland's local newspaper, opened with the headline: *"Trudy Harrison MP to champion Afghanistan vet safety"*.

Trudy had been part of the Operation Ark team from the very start due to several of her constituents who had contacted her via phone calls and email, raising concerns about our animal charity's plight and more specifically, the safety of our Afghan male and female vets and veterinary nurses. Trudy stated in the article by The News & Star, "I share their fears and have been working throughout the weekend with Pen Farthing – who runs the charity – to try to secure a safe passage to the UK."

It had been there all along in black and white. Neither the press nor any MP had bothered to do any research before commenting.

I had first met Trudy on the 15th of August in a Zoom meeting organised by Nina. I quickly typed a message to Nina. "Who is Trudy? Where did she come from?" as she was a random face not saying a lot but feverishly taking notes.

"Trudy Harrison, she is an MP," was the reply.

Trudy wrote the letter with her PPS signatory block to ensure we had an official-looking letter to show at Taliban checkpoints, immigration, or wherever it was bloody needed because *I asked her to.*

I could hardly rock up and show the Taliban a copy of Ben Wallace's tweet, could I?

I'd gone from being a distraction to being caught in the crossfire to being a bat to hit Boris with. Boris Johnson's enemies thought they'd found his downfall with this letter. Maybe other power brokers in this ecosystem realised how out of love the country was with him and wanted to replace him. In any case, it wasn't until June and Partygate that they finally managed to oust him.

There was no cloak-and-dagger stuff about Trudy's involvement. But there was such a collective craziness going on that I was forced to take a live interview with Channel Four news at 5pm one evening late in January 2022. This was an attempt to quell the rumours that I and Boris Johnson's wife, Carrie, were close friends and together we had plotted to pressure her husband to authorise dogs and cats and our staff to be airlifted from Kabul.

So once again for the record: we were not then and are not now friends. You will not find a photo of me and the Johnsons as I have never ever met them.

The news crew took over my living room here in Exeter. Lights and cameras were crammed in and the furniture moved around to accommodate it all. It was a veteran news reader who was going to be grilling me. We decided I needed a practise session with Nina and a few of the other team members to run over my answers. They had to be fluid and sound from the heart. As my microphone was fitted to the lapel of my freshly-ironed shirt just before we went live, I glanced up to see Kaisa in the doorway. Her beautiful blonde hair was still braided, ready for the day of climbing I'd promised her that had never materialised.

She never met my gaze. She drifted out to the garden whilst I was interviewed live.

The interview was a waste of time. Nothing changed. The press were still bashing Johnson about it and social media was still full of hate for me because of it.

I gave up.

June-August 2022

Towards the end of June 2022, Kaisa travelled back to Norway for a planned family party. After all, it was just an hour's flight from Gatwick.

She never came back.

My beautiful Kaisa. Who I adored and loved. Ended our relationship by text. I don't love you anymore.

She proceeded to cut ties with everyone who had known her during that period, even our close friends and family. It was as if she was erasing all memory of that period from her life.

The weeks after were just a blur. Tears, wine, rum, lots of rum mixed with more tears. Nothing else mattered as I stared at the screen of my silent phone and hoped beyond all hope, that it would burst into life with a message from my beloved Kaisa.

But none ever came.

Unable to focus or work, I took a leave of absence from the charity and went climbing in the Austrian Alps. With no partner to accompany me I climbed via ferrata, solo, no climbing rope to back me up. Just me, the guide wires, and the rock. Free to crimp my fingers around any available pro-truding flake of granite as my feet smeared against tiny edges.

Not for one moment did I feel scared. At that moment in my life, the hurt and extreme unpleasantness of everything I had just experienced, and the loss of Kaisa, led me to truly not care if it all ended there and then. Whether or not I made the summit was irrelevant. I was at peace with myself but not the world. I hated it.

As I pulled over the last steep edge of one climb onto the

ridge that led to the summit, I took in the majestic view with the glorious alpine valleys that stretched out beneath me.

Ahead two extremely fit and pleasant-looking ladies and their male guide were still packing away their climbing gear and ropes. I sensed the guide staring at me. I figured he had noticed my absence of technical equipment, which included the all-important harness.

In German, he asked me what time I had started. I looked at my watch before answering, and surprised myself.

"Twenty-two minutes ago," I answered in English. To be honest I couldn't be bothered to even humour him with a friendly gesture of an attempted reply in German. It dawned on me then that I was slightly out of breath.

I guess I had been climbing fairly fast.

All three looked completely taken aback. In a strong London twang one of the women responded, "That just took us four hours!" She was open mouthed and shaking her head.

"What can I say?" I smiled pleasantly as I replied. I took a swig from my bottle of "go" juice and surveyed the ground ahead. "I have a date at five o'clock."

A quick glance at my watch confirmed that it was now coming up to half past two in the afternoon and this was my second route of the day. I figured if I jogged briskly back down the descent path, I would have time for a dip in the crystal-blue lake I had spied on the way up and still be back in time for five o'clock.

I did have a date. Sadly not with some Alpine rock goddess but with a bottle of Austrian red and my favourite bar stool in the "Dorf" pub. That was all I cared about.

It was a stupid time. I was taking big risks and not really thinking through what would happen if I took just one misstep.

Sitting alone, propped up against the wooden bar in the remote alpine town of Neustift im Stubaital, my evenings were filled with red wine and remorse at everything to do with Operation Ark. I spoke to no one. Not even the chatty barmaid.

So many times whilst climbing I thought, what if I just ended it? Sitting high on an alpine ledge, legs dangling over the edge, nothing but hundreds of feet of air beneath them. One push and it would be over.

I could not see a way through the fog and confusion. I felt that life without Kaisa had no meaning. The torrent of abuse had really taken its toll. The ceaseless stress and the relentless negativity about everything good. The lies and the deceptions from people in power, whether in the House of Commons or elsewhere. The Royal Marine who had echoed them to young recruits. It was too much. The hatred dished out by all these elements left a void inside. I felt broken beyond repair.

This was beyond depression. This was a despair so total that I couldn't see how to live with it.

Many a time, high on those ledges I could easily have just let go. It would be simple and irreversible. I wondered, watching the fireball that brought life to this planet begin its slow descent behind the mountains to the west as shadows raced along the steep valleys below, if it would be the last sunset I would witness. The torment would be over.

Peace.

But deep down I knew it was not me, that was just something that I knew in my heart of hearts I would not do.

But it has given me a new perspective on those who do. Sometimes the overwhelming darkness is pretty powerful.

Thankfully, something kicked in for me at the top of the mountain. I couldn't give up.

On my last night in Neustift I decided to tell the charming young barmaid my sad story. I think she regretted pushing to chat to me. But I was just happy to talk about it all, talking helped even if she wasn't really listening. I recommend if you are ever in the place that I was in, find someone to talk to, even a working barmaid with poor English.

There were many lessons to be learnt from the life-changing withdrawal from Afghanistan. Sadly, I doubt any government of today will bother to. I've learned a lot, about myself and many more things beyond. And I'm still learning.

The Nowzad charity proved its determination and absolute commitment to its staff and core mission for animal welfare. We had done the right thing all along. I no longer put any thought into what people think of me. It has taken me a while to get to this stage. I have come to realise that it matters not if you tell somebody the world is round. If their view is that it is flat, then you are most likely wasting your breath.

And to be honest I truly no longer care. Life was far too short to be wasting it on dumbasses. I had a charity to rebuild and to build it better than it was before.

Part 5:
Epilogue

The smear campaign I endured has changed me. I am most definitely not the same person who started the charity. The events and aftermath of August 2021 have changed me. Even today, I truly struggle to comprehend the reasons why certain people lied about the events of those two weeks to the point of almost derailing Operation Ark and our charity. We had only ever tried to do our small part in supporting the rebuilding of Afghanistan. Of all the charities and people around the world to take down, why Nowzad? And why me?

I am still extremely disillusioned by it all. The aftermath of our successful Operation Ark came with too high a price and certain people have gone out of their way to make sure a price continues to be paid.

Anger.

Depression.

Bitterness.

Those feelings linger on, and I struggle most days to just get out of bed. Really, I do. Some no doubt will be quite happy to hear that. But I refuse to allow those hate-fuelled commentators to take anything away from what we eventually achieved with Operation Ark, especially for those young girls we evacuated.

They say time will heal. Hell, I sure hope it does. The truth must win in the end, right?

But regardless of what time eventually decides to do with me, there are some people I will never forgive.

There are some aspects of Operation Ark and the aftermath that will have to remain undisclosed. Too much hurt, sadness, and, I would assume from what I have already witnessed in the press, total lack of context if it was ever published, means that I don't want to go there. I can't. I could never understand the loathing that was directed towards me, a loathing that has never quite faded away. I lost friends and colleagues. I lost the love of my life. All because the British government was so grossly incompetent that it would rather have a man be dragged through the mud than admit their mistakes.

I had Nowzad and its supporters behind me, and I have a personality that keeps me fighting. I wonder how many others are thrown under the bus by the government and never get back up.

Considerations about the impact on Nowzad and the legal battle that would ensue if I included everything have also played a deciding factor for not including quite everything in this book. The charity is my life. I wouldn't do anything to hurt it.

–

Life threw another curveball at me a few months later.

With the Taliban leadership slowly transitioning to the functioning government of Afghanistan and mixed reports of the conditions on the ground, we had decided to hold off on attempting to re-establish Nowzad there. And besides, our beautiful small animal clinic was no more. With the Taliban leadership attempting to formalise the various factions flooding into Kabul, a random Taliban group had claimed our compound soon after we had evacuated. Dr Reshad had been forced to collect what equipment he could under gunpoint and vacate the premises with only two days' notice.

So we were not going back to Kabul anytime soon. We had no real idea how they would treat me as a former Marine and the instigator of Operation Ark, which had been for a time worldwide news.

We needed a new mission, something to focus the resources of the charity and, to be honest, our team. We were treading water.

I watched shocked, as I guess most people did, as Russia illegally invaded its neighbour, Ukraine, causing untold misery and loss of life.

Just like today, we had been scared that Putin was just crazy enough to press that big red button if cornered. The world watched as hundreds of thousands of Russian soldiers, conscripts, and former convicts were fed into the meat grinder of war by a compassionless dictator. And his unprovoked rhetoric had reinforced the notion that he might just press that button if he felt he was losing his grip on power.

The brave men and women of Ukraine surprised everyone with their determined defence as the West regrettably took far too long to support them with the much-needed weapons and ammunition to firstly halt the advance and then drive the Russians backwards.

I am extremely aware of what a nuclear war would bring. There would be no coming back from that. But I am also just very confused at the West's reluctance to stop a bully like Putin. Our dithering and the potential re-election of Donald Trump may well signal the end for Ukraine and usher in an emboldened Russia that we do not have the ability to deal with. It has not been lost on me that Trump could well signal the end of our charitable operations in yet another country.

As a charity we saw the need in Ukraine for what we do well: animal welfare in a hostile environment.

In April of 2022 I travelled out to Ukraine with some of our team to look at what we could set up and how we could do it. Nina and David accompanied me to the Polish-Ukrainian border. They looked at setting up a warehouse and office in Lviv, the largest city in western Ukraine, at the time flooded with refugees fleeing the destruction in the east and south of the country. Meanwhile, I headed towards Kyiv. I met up with an Aussie vet called Lach, and together we travelled into Irpin with a convoy of Ukrainian animal welfare groups organised by the Ukraine military.

The town, located just north of Bucha, had been mostly destroyed. It was the day after the Russian logistical supply chain had spectacularly failed, causing the forces threatening the capital Kyiv to retreat unceremoniously northwards back to Belarus. Destruction lay in every direction. We had come here to see for ourselves the need of the animal welfare groups as we went door to door looking for dogs still trapped in kennels as owners had fled, or cats locked inside houses with no food or water.

It was only as we were driving through that we realised some people had stayed behind.

"Over there." Lach pointed left through the passenger window of the nondescript white van I was driving. His finger-less gloves covered his hands as he indicated. I had to smile. The inside of the van was like an oven as he had cranked the heating up, causing me to strip down to just my thermal top. But as an Aussie veterinarian from the Sunshine Coast I guess the early Ukrainian spring weather was a little outside his normal operating climate.

My smile disappeared immediately as I clocked what he had seen. I pulled the van over.

Two very elderly Ukrainian gentlemen were bent over, struggling to stand upright whilst holding the load they had lifted from the floor between them. The object was awkwardly shaped, with no obvious grip. I immediately knew why it was too heavy. Too heavy for the elderly frames trying to lift it.

Lach had already exited the van and was walking over to offer his help.

I stayed sat in the van for a minute further. Just gripping the steering wheel. I looked ahead.

It was a body bag. And behind them along the road ahead there were many more. Just waiting to be collected.

I thought I had seen enough of war. I had come to Ukraine for the animal welfare issues, which I already knew were going to be emotional. I was prepared for that. Truly, I had not expected to just happen across bodies in the street. But then again neither had the Ukrainians as they retook the towns while the Russians fled. Nobody had expected atrocities on this scale.

Taking a deep breath, I dropped out of the van.

Together, we helped the two health workers load the bodies into the back of the old Soviet-era hearse that they were using. It was far too small for the task and we ended up having to load the bodies atop one another.

Even though we spoke no Ukrainian and the elderly gentlemen spoke no English, we all stood together for a minute in silence watching over the hearse. Then we all hugged and went on our separate ways. Lach and me for once driving in silence ourselves, the normal Aussie-Pom banter on hold for a while.

We had earlier that day rescued a Rottie dog from the confines of his outdoor kennel, the house adjacent to it utterly destroyed. I could not even begin to imagine the terror the dog had lived through whilst the bombs and missiles had rained down.

From the look of the dog, its ribs clear to be seen, it had

probably been trapped and uncared for in a kennel that had miraculously survived the destruction around it for likely two weeks, if not more. And this scenario was being repeated all over Bucha and Irpin as we discovered at the rendezvous point to hand over the dogs. The other teams were just as shocked and disturbed by the sights they were witnessing whilst searching their allocated areas.

Without doubt I knew that our charity could do some good here. With a determined team, the Nowzad charity opened a warehouse in Ukraine to provide animal shelters and animal welfare volunteers with the vital dog and cat food and medical supplies they needed to cater for the huge number of animals being abandoned or made homeless along the front lines of the conflict. In just a relatively short period of time we have supported the rabies vaccination of thousands of stray dogs and cats whilst helping to physically rebuild a shelter in Kramatorsk, eastern Ukraine, just an hour's drive from the current front line.

I had purpose again but sadly nobody to snuggle with at night. I did have Ragnar and Cora to keep me company when I was back in Britain, uncontrollably jumping up on me and doing their best to lick the life out of me as I collected them from kennels. Them having never been house-trained in Kabul before coming to England meant that I had so much fun as they adapted to living in a proper house. NOT.

Soon and without really knowing how it happened, they gained themselves a new four-legged buddy called Leif, and much to my resignation, have claimed my sofa as theirs. If you were to ever come to my house for tea, be prepared to sit on hardback wooden chairs, the dogs will be lounging on *their* sofa.

In July of 2022 I finished a call with Dr Reshad, our vet who had stayed behind to continue to manage the donkey sanctuary. We had finally decided it was now safe enough for me to return to the place I once called home.

And for me, a Westerner with a British passport, it was actually not as stressful as I had imagined.

The same people manned the immigration desk, customs, security checkpoints. They just wore more traditional Afghan clothing. The Western uniforms were now long gone. Nobody asked me any problematic questions as I was being processed. My dread at returning soon dissipated.

Non-governmental organisations are left alone to operate their humanitarian programmes, although we had to re-register with all the relevant authorities again, which was a very stressful and at times, a very frustrating process.

Working with our new vet team on the ground, re-establishing Nowzad's presence in Kabul has been hard work. But together we were determined to continue the vital animal welfare work that is needed daily in the streets of Afghanistan, which are sadly now even harsher.

As we were evicted from our previous compound, we are now operating from a brand-new facility in central Kabul at the request of the current government of Afghanistan. Nowzad is proud to have opened the first ever twenty-four-hour animal hospital in Kabul. Our donkey sanctuary has expanded to provide an in-depth working animal programme to support the overworked and abused donkeys and horses on the streets of Kabul, and the surrounding area. The team are back in schools showing young Afghan children how to treat an animal with compassion and kindness. We have no female vets. We have to work within the rules of the new government.

What the rest of the world thinks about Afghanistan is not something I have much say in. And I definitely cannot change any government policy. I'll leave it to them and just keep working with Nowzad to make the small changes that our charity can do to prevent the spread of rabies and to support animal welfare.

I don't live in Kabul full-time anymore, just travel in and out as needed. Home is now definitely back in England with the dogs.

I have no idea what the future has in store for me. But then again, who does?

To find out more about the Nowzad charity please visit **www.nowzad.com** especially if you would like to donate.

Thank you for caring.

Acknowledgments

This book was almost never written as none of my previous publishers would take the story. They told me I was too toxic.

I almost gave up.

But then a supporter of our Nowzad charity, called Pamela, emailed me to suggest a small independent publisher called Claret Press.

And the rest as they say is history... Thank you Katie Isbester for taking the gamble and believing in the true story of Operation Ark and for supporting me to bring out the vision I had for this book. You have helped me with the healing process that was so desperately needed. And you are not too bad for a boss whilst we did the edits – I think we worked well together!

The rest of the Claret Press team have been instrumental in supporting the publication of this book. Thank you to Alexander Green for your editorial assistance and fine suggestions – I agree with you, we should have kept the Porta-John toilet episode in.

Thank you Petya Tsankova for the amazing book cover, it definitely reflects the story within. And I am looking forward to working more closely with Ines Palmer, the rights manager as we publish around the world!

I knew what I wanted to write but not all of what I wanted to say was suitable nor did I have the word count. Thank you to El Niño for reading all of my initial manuscripts and then working with me on what to keep and what to let go of. And for just being a sounding board as I ranted or laughed at the absurdity of it all. Not sure if you realise just how much you have helped me to move on, but you have, and you have made me smile so much along the way. (The rum and cokes and maybe a PiiM are on me next time.)

And to all who buy this book and read the true story of what happened during those few weeks of utter chaos and madness in Afghanistan during August 2021, I need the truth to be out there and you are helping me to do that. Thank you.

Pen
July 2024

GREAT STORYTELLING
DOESN'T JUST ENTERTAIN,
IT ENERGISES

Claret Press' mission is simple: we publish engrossing books which engage with the issues of the day. So we publish across a range of genres, both fiction and nonfiction. From award-winning page-turners to eye-opening travelogues, from captivating historical fiction to insightful memoirs, there's a Claret Press book for you.

To keep up to date about the going-ons at Claret Press, including book launches, Zoom talks and other events, sign up to our newsletter through our website at:

www.claretpress.com

You can also find us through Instagram **@claretpress** Twitter **@ClaretPress** and TikTok **@claret.press**

Claret Press